Sounds Like a New Woman

A DECADE OF

NEW WOMEN AND

THUMPS ON THE HEAD

Sounds Like a

From the Editors of **NewWoman** Magazine

PENGUIN BOOKS

Editor: Jody L. Rohlena
Picture editor: Lisa Ilario

PENGUIN BOOKS
Published by the Penguin Group
Penguin Books USA Inc., 375 Hudson Street,
New York, New York 10014, U.S.A.
Penguin Books Ltd, 27 Wrights Lane, London W8 5TZ, England
Penguin Books Australia Ltd, Ringwood, Victoria, Australia
Penguin Books Canada Ltd, 10 Alcorn Avenue,
Toronto, Ontario, Canada M4V 3B2
Penguin Books (N.Z.) Ltd, 182–190 Wairau Road,
Auckland 10, New Zealand

Penguin Books Ltd, Registered Offices:
Harmondsworth, Middlesex, England

First published in Penguin Books 1993

10 9 8 7 6 5 4 3 2 1

Copyright © K-III Magazine Corporation, A Delaware Corporation, 1993
All rights reserved

Photograph credits appear on page 84.

ISBN 0 14 01.7636 5

Printed in the United States of America
Set in Bodoni Book
Designed by Jessica Shatan

Except in the United States of America, this book is sold subject to the condition that it shall not, by way of trade or otherwise, be lent, re-sold, hired out, or otherwise circulated without the publisher's prior consent in any form of binding or cover other than that in which it is published and without a similar condition including this condition being imposed on the subsequent purchaser.

Acknowledgments

Thanks are due to many *New Woman* employees, both past and present, for their help in bringing this book to print. First, I'm grateful to Susan Kane, who supervised every aspect of this project from the very beginning; to Jody Rohlena, for her editorial research, judgment, and writing; to Lisa Ilario, for her photo research; to Dirk Vonderlage and Debra Birnbaum, for their editorial efforts; and to all the editors who have ever worked on the magazine's Attitudes (better known as "Sounds Like a New Woman/A Thump on the Head to") page.

I'm indebted to Mindy Werner, the book's editor, for her endless patience and good humor.

Most of all, I want to acknowledge all the wonderful *New Woman* readers who have sent quotes to the Attitudes page for publication year after year. Without them, our magazine, its most famous page, and this book simply would not exist.

KAREN WALDEN
New Woman
Editor-in-chief
September 1993

Introduction

The Pill. *The Feminine Mystique*. The National Organization for Women. *The Mary Tyler Moore Show*. We all know what these things have in common—they had a significant impact on women's lives in the 1960s and early 1970s.

This was a period of enormous change and growth for women—a period that, fortunately, hasn't ended yet. More and more women were entering previously male-dominated fields, and, in their relationships with men, they were asserting their needs and declaring their independence. These women were all ages and all colors; they were from all backgrounds and all geographic areas. The one thing they shared was an *attitude*. They believed women had the strength and the talent to do and be anything they wanted.

Enter *New Woman*, a magazine launched in 1970 to celebrate that attitude. We found the "New Woman attitude" in women—and in men—everywhere. And we found just as many people who didn't share our views. We wanted to provide a forum for all of the voices of the new era. So in 1972 we started a column of celebrity quotes—for a fun and illuminating look at the attitudes of a new generation.

We divided the quotes into three sections: "Swap the Old Lady . . ." (for less-than-liberated comments), "For a New Woman" (for the forward-thinking of our role models), and "A Thump on the Head to . . ." (for patently sexist points of view).

The column quickly became the readers' favorite. It has evolved over the last two decades, as has the rest of the magazine, and today we call the page, simply, Attitudes. It is our signature page, the magazine in shorthand—because it is here where we most clearly define who is a New Woman . . . and who is *not!*

The column has been running for more than two decades. What you'll find here are the most enlightening New Woman quotes and the most outrageous Thump quotes of the last decade: 1983–1993. You won't see any "Old Ladies," though; we eliminated that category in 1989 when we decided that to call anyone an old lady was contrary to the magazine's motto: "A New Woman is an attitude, not an age."

You'll be surprised when you compare quotes from the early years with quotes from the later years. In many cases, we have indeed "come a long way, baby." And in other cases, it seems the more things change the more they stay the same. Some people never learn. You'll see a number of "repeat offenders" here—people who practically beg us to thump them for the scandalous things they just keep saying, year after year. In fact, we have something of a Thump Hall of Fame (or should we say Hall of Shame?)—a special distinction for the three-timers in this book: Don Johnson, Gene Simmons, Charles Barkley, Jerry Falwell, Pat Robertson, and Ted Turner. President of the Hall of Shame: Phyllis Schlafly, with a record four thumps.

But on the bright side, other people inspire us by appearing again and again on the "Sounds Like a New Woman" portion of the page. Our hats are off to those enlightened souls who continue to speak out, continue to question the status quo, continue to raise our consciousness. These New Women have many different faces: Whoopi Goldberg, Robert Redford, Barbra Streisand, Linda Ellerbee, Michael Jordan, Miss Piggy. To all of you New Women out there, keep it up! We're counting on you—not just to fill our pages but to better our world.

That goes for the New Women who read our magazine as well. We rely on them to supply us with the quotes that make up our Attitudes page each month. Our editors choose the mix of the good, the bad, and the downright ugly. And we always make sure the quotes are accurate and from reliable sources. But the process begins with the readers of *New Woman* magazine.

The voices in this book reveal the attitudes men and women are most passionate about—for better and for worse. On the "Thump" side of the page, you'll read a lot about how women should stay out of male-dominated professions (like sports, sports refereeing, and politics, to name a few), how they should keep their mouths shut and their men happy in bed. And on the "New Woman" side, you'll read about women doing and being whatever and whomever they want—umpires, heads of state, single mothers, business leaders. New Women also love and respect themselves—wrinkles, generous hips, and all. They don't view growing older as the beginning of the end, but as a new beginning. They love life and have a passionate involvement in it. They prove that a feminist can be any age, any gender, any race, any religion. (And our Thumpees prove that a sexist can, too.)

You will surely notice that some people's attitudes have changed since the time they were quoted (as have their appearances and occupations; the IDs in the book describe each person in the year that he or she was quoted, and the photos are of approximately the same vintage). For example, on the "Sounds Like a New Woman" pages, you'll hear celebrities make loving comments about spouses to whom they are no longer married. Others bounce from "New Woman" to "Thump" and vice versa. History will be the judge as to which sentiments hold true for the long haul.

The same is true for "Thump" quotes that may sound as though they were made in jest. Only the Thumpees know whether they were kidding or not. But our feeling is that mean-spirited comments are never all in fun. And maybe if people know that we're out there, listening to the things they say, even when they think no one is paying attention, they might just be a little more careful!

From here on out, the quotes speak for themselves. You're sure to be enlightened and amazed, shocked and inspired, thrilled and chilled. Read on . . . and enjoy!

Sounds Like a New Woman

1983–1985

A decade ago, several New Women emerged who spoke their minds and continue to speak for women today: Oprah Winfrey, who catapulted to national fame from a local Chicago talk show; Cher, whose inspired (and inspiring) performances in *Silkwood* (1983) and *Mask* (1985) showed that she was more than just Sonny's ex; and Madonna, who has reinvented herself a dozen times over since her early "Material Girl" days and has become as visible as she is controversial. Today all three of these women are one-word household names. You'll see "Sounds Like a New Woman" quotes from each of them in the years 1983–1985 (and again in later years).

Likewise, people who were earning themselves a "Thump on the Head" back then still appear on our pages today. For example, antifeminist Phyllis Schlafly appears in this book in 1984, 1985, 1988, and 1993.

Some other names to look for in these next "Thump" pages (and throughout the book): Ted Turner, whose best communications come via satellite, not out of his mouth; Barbara Cartland, who is *not* one of the great feminist writers of all time; and Gene Simmons, former lead singer of the rock group Kiss (is it any wonder his romance with Cher didn't last?).

And who would have thought that Jane Fonda, a New Woman in 1984, would later wind up with Thump King Ted Turner?

By contrast, Mick Jagger and Jerry Hall would seem to be a match made in heaven—if outmoded ideas about a woman's role in the family are any indication of overall compatibility. Look for his and her "Thump" quotes in 1985. Mick said he would marry then-girlfriend Jerry "when she presents me with a son." Well, they have since had a son and gotten married—although it seems it hasn't been complete "satisfaction" since they tied the knot.

1983

"After all these years, I am still involved in the process of self-discovery. It's better to explore life and make mistakes than to play it safe. Mistakes are part of the dues one pays for a full life."

SOPHIA LOREN, ACTOR

"It's marvelous that Jane Fonda and Raquel Welch can show how superb one can look at forty. But who ever thought about Margaret Mead's looks? Or Mother Teresa's beauty, which lies in an older face lit with intelligence, a mouth that shows compassion? The media should point out women who are beautiful because of their great mental and intellectual achievements, too."

LIV ULLMANN, ACTOR

"There is a growing strength in women—but it's in the forehead, not the forearm."

BEVERLY SILLS, OPERA SINGER

"I simply ache from smiling. Why are women expected to beam all the time? It's unfair. If a man looks solemn, it's automatically assumed he's a serious person, not a miserable one."

QUEEN ELIZABETH II, ABOUT BEING CRITICIZED FOR HER SERIOUS EXPRESSION

"It's better, I think, to be complimented on your talent than your looks. At least I had some small say in developing that . . ."

CATHERINE DENEUVE, ACTOR

"The term 'working mother' is redundant."

ERMA BOMBECK, HUMOR COLUMNIST

1983

"Henry VIII . . . he didn't get divorced, he just had [his wives'] heads chopped off when he got tired of them. That's a good way to get rid of a woman—no alimony!"
TED TURNER, COMMUNICATIONS MAGNATE

"At some stage in life, friendship with a woman becomes more and more important, but I haven't reached that stage yet. I don't think of women as friends—I always think of them in terms of romance and lust."
ED MARINARO, ACTOR

"I don't want a woman who has anything of magnitude or devastating interest to say."
DUDLEY MOORE, ACTOR

"There's only two things you people are good for: Having kids and frying bacon."
BOBBY KNIGHT, INDIANA UNIVERSITY BASKETBALL COACH, ABOUT WOMEN

"When I'm with a man, my work takes second place—all I really want to do is get through the day so I can rush home to be with him. That's because my man is the most important part of my life."
LINDA EVANS, ACTOR

"Why is it men are permitted to be obsessed about their work, but women are only permitted to be obsessed about men?"
BARBRA STREISAND, SINGER

"I believe people should bear aging. Women get a nice look when they start to experience things and so do men."
ROBERT REDFORD, ACTOR

"Women share with men the need for personal success, even the taste for power, and no longer are we willing to satisfy those needs through the achievements of surrogates, whether husbands, children, or merely role models."
ELIZABETH DOLE, U.S. SECRETARY OF TRANSPORTATION

"I'm forty-six years old, and if you look at the history of aging actresses, it's not exactly a bright future. I intend, of course, to change that."
JANE FONDA, ACTOR

"My mother told me, 'Never call boys on the telephone. Let them take the first step.' If I'd done that, I'd probably be somebody's secretary right now instead of secretary of state."
SUSAN FARMER, RHODE ISLAND SECRETARY OF STATE

"Whether you're married or not, whether you have a boyfriend or not, there is no real security except for whatever you build inside yourself."
GILDA RADNER, ACTOR

1984

"You should not be an actress. Get married instead and have a baby."
CARY GRANT, ACTOR, TO A FEMALE ACTOR HE WAS DATING

"I feel a woman should never stand when she can sit and never sit when she can lie. Everything is much easier that way."
BARBARA CARTLAND, AUTHOR

"The ERA was born about sixty years ago. For about fifty years Congress had the good sense to leave it in the bottom drawer."
PHYLLIS SCHLAFLY, PRESIDENT OF THE EAGLE FORUM

"To manufacture only small sizes is a favor for humanity. I prevent ugly girls from showing off their bad figures."
ELIO FIORUCCI, FASHION DESIGNER

"Girls who are worth taking out are those who like food. You know what will follow will be more or less of the same order. When you go out with a woman and she says, 'I don't drink wine,' already an alarm bell rings."
ROMAN POLANSKI, MOVIE DIRECTOR

1985

"It's an experience every man should have. We don't know what a woman goes through. We just sit back after it's all over and pass out cigars and say, 'See what I did.'"
BEN VEREEN, ACTOR, ABOUT WITNESSING CHILDBIRTH

> "The marriages I've seen work best are those in which both husband and wife take pride in their mate's accomplishments."
> **SHELLEY LONG, ACTOR**

"The thing women must do to rise to power is redefine their femininity. Once, power was considered a masculine attribute. In fact, power has no sex."
KATHARINE GRAHAM, CHAIRPERSON AND CEO OF THE WASHINGTON POST COMPANY

"I hope it will open doors for stories about women who have attractive souls and not just attractive bodies."
TYNE DALY, ACTOR, WHEN ASKED WHAT HOPES SHE HAD FOR TV AFTER WINNING AN EMMY

"I'm glad to have a girl-following, because I want to encourage them. I try to beget strength and courage and purpose. I want to show a new woman."
CYNDI LAUPER, SINGER

"My happiness doesn't come from outside anymore—not from an award or a guy or this or that. The 'perk' of going through any catastrophic event in your life is that you discover happiness. True happiness comes from within."
EILEEN BRENNAN, ACTOR, ABOUT HER BRUSH WITH DEATH AFTER BEING HIT BY A CAR

1985

"If you get married, sex is part of the contract."
STATE REPRESENTATIVE PATRICIA HILL (REPUBLICAN, TEXAS), ABOUT WHY SHE VOTED AGAINST A BILL THAT MAKES SPOUSAL RAPE A CRIME

"I've always felt the man is king of the house and should be amused and treated well."
JERRY HALL, MODEL

"When she presents me with a son."
MICK JAGGER, SINGER, IN RESPONSE TO A QUESTION ABOUT WHEN HE PLANS TO MARRY HIS GIRLFRIEND, MODEL JERRY HALL

"I think the ideal family is four—two boys and two girls. That way you can mess up with one boy and still have a chance of the other one turning out all right."
JIMMY OSMOND, SINGER

"Women who tell me they don't want husbands and children—there is some psychic damage there somewhere. They've been turned off the true course."
ANITA BROOKNER, AUTHOR

"I'm not a feminist. I believe woman was made for man. Feminism just isn't important to me."
KIM ALEXIS, MODEL

1985

"A mature woman doesn't have to push, and she doesn't have to depend on gimmicks or beauty aids. It's her attitude toward life that makes her mature and attractive."

PAUL NEWMAN, ACTOR

"Empathy is the single most revolutionary emotion I can think of. Women and men can understand each other if they think themselves into the other person's situation."

KIRSTIE ALLEY, ACTOR

"I resent the idea that you can't be both sexy and smart. When I dyed my hair, the peroxide didn't fry my brain cells."

LONI ANDERSON, ACTOR

"History will judge that the decision to pick the first woman to run on the national ticket of either party was a bold and proper step that strengthened our nation."

FORMER VICE PRESIDENT WALTER MONDALE ABOUT HIS 1984 PRESIDENTIAL CAMPAIGN

"A man can be called ruthless if he bombs a country into oblivion. A woman can be called ruthless if she puts you on hold."

GLORIA STEINEM, FOUNDING EDITOR OF MS. MAGAZINE

"I would like to see women stop dressing, either consciously or unconsciously, for a man. To dress for themselves—not for some man in their bedroom or their boardroom."

GAYLE PERKINS, FASHION DESIGNER

"I'm tough, ambitious, and I know exactly what I want. If that makes me a bitch, okay."

MADONNA, SINGER

1985

"Never attend a party without a good-looking woman, even if she's your sister or you have to borrow her for the evening."

JULIO IGLESIAS, SINGER

"I cook occasionally just to see how easy women's work is."

THOMAS P. O'NEILL, SPEAKER OF THE HOUSE OF REPRESENTATIVES

"Educating a woman is like pouring honey over a fine Swiss watch. It stops working."

KURT VONNEGUT, JR., AUTHOR

"Women are taking the man out of their men, and I don't like that. A woman needs a man whom she can't control."

LORETTA LYNN, SINGER

"Sexual harassment on the job is not a problem for the virtuous woman."

PHYLLIS SCHLAFLY, PRESIDENT OF THE EAGLE FORUM

"The Jacksonville Recreation and Parks Department will sponsor youth and adult tennis lessons starting in July. The fee for women and youth lessons is $20 and the fee for lessons for men is $10."

JACKSONVILLE, FLORIDA, RECREATION AND PARKS DEPARTMENT

1985

"Remember, Ginger Rogers did everything Fred Astaire did, but she did it backward and in high heels."
FAITH WHITTLESEY, WHITE HOUSE AIDE, ABOUT THE CHALLENGE OF BEING A WOMAN ON THE PRESIDENT'S STAFF

"We never wanted to be popular and successful because we were women. We wanted to be successful and popular and be women."
JANE WIEDLIN, GUITARIST FOR THE GO-GO'S

"We don't see that many of our male stars' frontal nudity. It makes me uncomfortable to be in an unequal position."
MERYL STREEP, ACTOR, ABOUT WHY SHE'S RELUCTANT TO DO NUDE SCENES

"Women have just as much right to an uninterrupted career as men, and fathers have just as much responsibility as mothers for caring for their children or deciding who will care for them."
DR. BENJAMIN SPOCK, CHILD-CARE EXPERT

"I have a lot of friends who are bringing up their children alone. Men are not a necessity. You don't need them to live. You don't have to have them to survive."
CHER, ACTOR

1985

"Women—they have to be nice-looking. But men—they must be smart."

IVANA TRUMP, FORMER MODEL AND WIFE OF ENTREPRENEUR DONALD TRUMP

"I think it's natural for a man to be promiscuous . . . and you're talking to a guy who's just following his natural instincts."

GENE SIMMONS, ROCK SINGER

"I think I'm more [financially] responsible than [my wife] is. But isn't that the way it usually is?"

MIKE LYNN, MINNESOTA VIKINGS GENERAL MANAGER

"Basically, I don't think that a lot of the women have enough experiences to draw from. That's why it seems there's always more men than women in comedy."

JAMES BELUSHI, ACTOR, ABOUT WOMEN COMEDIANS

"The only way to resolve a situation with a girl is to jump on her, and things will work out."

LEE MARVIN, ACTOR

"A woman who has never been hit by a man has never been loved."

ZSA ZSA GABOR, ACTOR

1986–1988

There are certain types of people who seem to earn "thumps" over and over again: sports figures (particularly baseball players, although we've never quite figured out why), actors and politicians (both of whom are quoted so frequently they have countless opportunities to insert their feet into their mouths), and televangelists (although several of the most vocal spokesmen have since been "dethroned").

To be fair, though, for every thumped actor or politician, there's always a New Woman—or two or three. Unfortunately, the same isn't always true for sports figures and evangelists.

You'll see all of your favorite holy rollers in the next few pages: Jerry Falwell, Jimmy Swaggart, Pat Robertson, and Tammy Faye Bakker, who said she "loves to be under submission" to her husband, Jim Bakker.

Other people, people we like to think of as New Women, disappoint when they end up on the "Thump" side of the page. Some examples from these next few years: Katharine Hepburn, who says she thinks every woman needs a man to look up to; and Joan Baez, who says to actor Don Johnson, "Could we discuss the possibility of rape?"

And there are some folks who simply defy categorization. Several of our most notorious Thumpees have appeared on the other half of the page, as New Women; and several promising New Women have lapsed and landed in the "Thump" column. Watch for the waffling of Delta Burke, Corbin Bernsen, and Arnold Schwarzenegger. (He earns his first Thump on the Head in 1986, then redeems himself in 1991, but regresses again in 1992.) Other wafflers will appear in later years as well.

1986

"I reject the compliment. One either thinks or doesn't, regardless of sex."

FORMER U.S. REPRESENTATIVE CLARE BOOTHE LUCE (REPUBLICAN, CONNECTICUT), RESPONDING TO A COLLEAGUE'S REMARK THAT SHE HAD A "MASCULINE MIND"

"I cannot understand why someone would not choose life over the loss of a breast. . . . Life is worth it."

ANN JILLIAN, ACTOR, ABOUT HER DOUBLE MASTECTOMY

"I'm interested in people, nice people—not America's sexiest women."

MARK HARMON, ACTOR, WHOM *PEOPLE* MAGAZINE NAMED AMERICA'S SEXIEST MAN

"I would rather be by myself at home than with a man whose company I did not enjoy."

STEPHANIE ZIMBALIST, ACTOR

"I'd go for that. She'd make a great president."

U.S. SENATOR ROBERT DOLE (REPUBLICAN, KANSAS), RESPONDING TO AN ADMIRER WHO SUGGESTED DOLE AND HIS WIFE, U.S. SECRETARY OF TRANSPORTATION ELIZABETH DOLE, FORM A DOLE AND DOLE TICKET IN 1988

"If American women would increase their voting turnout by ten percent, I think we would see an end to all of the budget cuts in programs benefiting women and children."

CORETTA SCOTT KING, WIDOW OF MARTIN LUTHER KING, JR.

1986

"When you watch wrestling, you boo and holler and you don't have to beat up your wife and kids to get your frustrations out."

MR. T., ACTOR

"The ultimate authority needs to be the husband."

PAT ROBERTSON, EVANGELIST

"I can cat around a bit, but she can't."

ERIC DICKERSON, L.A. RAMS RUNNING BACK, ABOUT HIS GIRLFRIEND

"Right now, the issues are being ignored because Nebraska is running this state prom queen contest and calling it a governor's race."

STATE SENATOR JOHN DECAMP (REPUBLICAN, NEBRASKA), ABOUT HIS STATE'S GUBERNATORIAL RACE BETWEEN TWO FEMALE CANDIDATES

"We will never have the place of men. It is our role to bring peace, to bring order, to bring passion, to bring beauty."

IMELDA MARCOS, WIFE OF DEPOSED PHILIPPINE PRESIDENT FERDINAND MARCOS, ABOUT FILIPINO WOMEN

"She goes to the games and sits with the players' wives, who also think they know something about the game—but they just gossip."

DENNIS HARRAH, L.A. RAMS GUARD, COMMENTING ON HIS GIRLFRIEND'S ATTENDANCE AT FOOTBALL GAMES

1986

"I've always believed that one woman's success can only help another woman's success."
GLORIA VANDERBILT, FASHION DESIGNER

"Why would you want to base your image on anything as transitory as your looks? I'd like people to think of beauty as not being physical."
KELLY MCGILLIS, ACTOR

"To me, the greatest Latin lover was my dad, who married my mother and was faithful to her until the day he died, fifty-five years later."
RICARDO MONTALBAN, ACTOR

"I much prefer brains to curves in women. Honesty, courage, and a sensible outlook are traits I find appealing."
TED DANSON, ACTOR

"A passionate interest in what you do is the secret of enjoying life, perhaps the secret of long life, whether it is helping old people or children, or making cheese, or growing earthworms."
JULIA CHILD, CHEF

1986

"Maria is getting the professional drive out of the way. After that she will be satisfied to be a mother."

ARNOLD SCHWARZENEGGER, ACTOR, ABOUT HIS FIANCÉE, TV JOURNALIST MARIA SHRIVER

"A successful man makes more money than his wife can spend. A successful woman is one who can find such a man."

LANA TURNER, ACTOR

"A woman who teases deserves rape."

GEORGE HAMILTON, ACTOR

"I know it's a sexist opinion, but I hold it nonetheless: women do not park as well as men."

ANDY ROONEY, 60 MINUTES COMMENTATOR

"Be quiet. Didn't your husband teach you not to interrupt when a man is talking?"

PIETER BOTHA, PRESIDENT OF SOUTH AFRICA, RESPONDING TO A FEMALE HECKLER

"You know how women are. They get crazy at times and yell a lot."

JIM BROWN, FOOTBALL HALL OF FAMER, ABOUT BEING ARRESTED ON SUSPICION OF ASSAULTING HIS FIANCÉE

"Show me a person who has never made a mistake and I'll show you somebody who has never achieved much."
JOAN COLLINS, ACTOR

"In my opinion, there are no women's issues, only issues which affect women more than men. But I believe all issues are women's issues, or should be."
MARTHA LAYNE COLLINS, GOVERNOR OF KENTUCKY

"I don't view being single as some sort of waiting period between marriages. For me it is a genuine alternative to marriage. I am quite happily single."
CYBILL SHEPHERD, ACTOR

"The recognition by men that women are co-custodians of this planet, although absurdly belated, is one of the most hopeful developments in recent history."
CARL SAGAN, ASTRONOMER

"As I see it, a guy can be sensitive and not be a wimp."
JUDGE REINHOLD, ACTOR

"I'll make some concessions if the request is reasonable. But I'm in this deal because I'm valued from the neck up. If someone tells me to comb my hair, I'll comb my hair. If someone tells me to dye it blond, they can go to hell."
JANE WALLACE, CBS NEWS CORRESPONDENT

"The Roman Empire immediately before its collapse—you'll find the same idiotic things they were doing we're doing today, including lesbianism, homosexuality, women participating in the running of the government . . ."
DON AMECHE, ACTOR

"I'm aware that a large part of our audience is sex-starved females. And to hear females tell it, they're all sex-starved."
DON JOHNSON, ACTOR, ABOUT HIS SUCCESSFUL TV SHOW *MIAMI VICE*

"Feminists hate men, that's the problem."
JERRY FALWELL, FOUNDER OF THE MORAL MAJORITY

"The patience of a saint, spunk, and a head flat enough to set a can of beer on."
ROBERT HAYS, ACTOR, ABOUT WHAT HE LOOKS FOR IN A WOMAN

"Humbleness and insecurity make a woman lovely to look at."
GEORGE MASTERS, MAKEUP ARTIST TO THE RICH AND FAMOUS

"I think [tennis] is tough enough on a man, and I would like other things in her future—dance and ballet and all the things that little girls do."
JIMMY CONNORS, TENNIS CHAMP, ABOUT WHETHER HE WOULD LIKE HIS DAUGHTER TO PLAY PROFESSIONAL TENNIS SOMEDAY

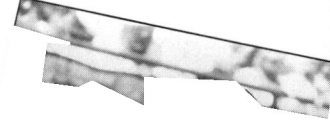

1987

"I'm not panicked about marriage. If I marry, I marry; if I don't, I don't. I'm not thinking about it now, because I love my work. I have good friends."

SUSAN SEIDELMAN, MOVIE DIRECTOR

"I don't play the womanizer. I'm the lover of womanhood."

BARRY BOSTWICK, ACTOR

"I've always had a little contempt for women who marry because they want to be looked after in their old age. I always thought one should be rich oneself."

ANJELICA HUSTON, ACTOR

"Youth is in the mind, not in the condition of your flesh."

GINGER ROGERS, DANCER

"Who was it who said, 'A man of quality is never threatened by a woman of equality'? Marianne obviously can't base her life on having me around."

KENNY ROGERS, SINGER, ABOUT HIS WIFE'S NEW SINGING CAREER

"You're not a man if you can make a baby, you're only a man if you can raise a baby."

THE REVEREND JESSE JACKSON, FOUNDER OF THE RAINBOW COALITION

1987

"There's something you can get from a chick that you can't have with any other being on the planet, and that is something super special. I mean, if there were nothing but old whores and nasty, old, hard-looking women, I'd be out looking for some young, sweet, little fifteen-year-old boy."
DON JOHNSON, ACTOR

"I enjoy getting dressed as a Barbie doll."
VANNA WHITE, CO-HOST OF THE TV SHOW WHEEL OF FORTUNE

"*Platoon* was magnificent, but it's just so catastrophic. They should have had a sign outside that said, 'No Women Allowed.'"
MICKEY ROONEY, ACTOR

"Damn it, when you get married, you kind of expect you're going to get a little sex."
FORMER U.S. SENATOR JEREMIAH DENTON (REPUBLICAN, ALABAMA), ABOUT WHY HE OPPOSED A STRENGTHENED LAW AGAINST SPOUSAL RAPE

"Liberated women are going to rain down on me, but, as old-fashioned as it sounds, if an important decision has to be made, I let Gary [my husband] make it."
AMY GRANT, SINGER

"I haven't changed that many diapers. A few, just a few. I don't consider that my job."
NICK NOLTE, ACTOR

1987

"They say getting thin is the best revenge. Success is much better."

OPRAH WINFREY, TALK SHOW HOST

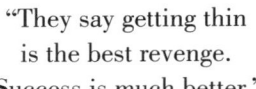

"I do not lead in a masculine manner. I lead as a woman. You can be a woman leader, a feminine leader, and still be strong."

GENERAL EVA BURROWS, HEAD OF THE SALVATION ARMY

"I always stop working in September, because as a father, I want to be more than a visitor."

TED NUGENT, ROCK SINGER

"I really feel terrific about my wrinkles. I'm comfortable with them and I believe I would look most peculiar if I didn't have them. If I had my face pulled tight, I'd lose my identity."

ANGELA LANSBURY, ACTOR

"People are always saying, 'There was never a black figure skater before. What motivated you?' I didn't have to have a black figure skater to motivate me. My mom always led me to believe I could do whatever I wanted to do."

DEBI THOMAS, WORLD CHAMPION FIGURE SKATER

"She captivated me with her beauty and charm and brains and alienated me with her nagging. Of course, if she makes me mad, I'll shoot her."
DARRYL DAWKINS, NEW JERSEY NETS CENTER, ABOUT HIS WIFE, KELLY

"I think a woman should stay home and take care of her children. It's inexcusable for a woman to let her career become that important."
CHRISSIE HYNDE, LEAD SINGER OF THE PRETENDERS, ABOUT BALANCING CAREER AND FAMILY

"I don't think the choice between a job and a child is unfair. It's simply reality, and many women have made the choice. Because of biology, women will never be equal."
STATE REPRESENTATIVE COLLEEN ENGLER (REPUBLICAN, MICHIGAN), ABOUT WHY SHE IS AGAINST GOVERNMENT-MANDATED MATERNITY LEAVE

"I think women have ruined the Democratic party. The Democratic party has had candidates throughout the last twelve years who were about as rousing as oatmeal. And one of the reasons is that no man can rise in the Democratic party now who doesn't say 'women first.'"
NORMAN MAILER, AUTHOR

"There's plenty of ways to cover a full hip. One of them is to stay in bed."
EARL BLACKWELL, FASHION ARBITER

"I don't cook. I have a woman."
RYAN O'NEAL, ACTOR

1987

"I'm hooked on fatherhood. If I were to list the happiest moments of my life, the births of my children would be right up there on top."

MEL GIBSON, ACTOR

"I don't like to be labeled as lonely just because I'm alone."

DELTA BURKE, ACTOR

"There is not a man shortage. There is actually a man excess. Look at the House of Representatives. Look at the Senate. Look at the tenured faculty in any American college. You will see an appalling man excess, which means a woman shortage."

BARBARA EHRENREICH, AUTHOR

"Don't settle for 'We've got *Cagney & Lacey*, we've got a woman on the Supreme Court. . . .' You get equality by being equal and never settling for less. Ever."

LINDA ELLERBEE, JOURNALIST

"When I was ten, I was told somebody's got to clean the fish. Well, my idea of feminism is that everyone cleans the fish."

CYNDI LAUPER, SINGER

1987

"When people congratulate me, I show them the [engagement] ring. They're talking about the series, but I say, 'Let's get our priorities straight. I got a man.'"
JEAN SMART, ACTOR ON THE TV SHOW DESIGNING WOMEN

"It's hard to find a fifty-year-old woman that a younger guy will fall in love with."
ELMORE LEONARD, AUTHOR, ABOUT FINDING A LEAD ACTRESS FOR THE MOVIE VERSION OF HIS BOOK *LA BRAVA*

"Governor [James] Thompson can't say no. If he were a female, he'd be pregnant."
FORMER U.S. SENATOR ADLAI E. STEVENSON III (DEMOCRAT, ILLINOIS)

"I love being under submission to my husband."
TAMMY FAYE BAKKER, WIFE OF EVANGELIST JIM BAKKER

"It's easier to be stupid and to laugh [with men]. With a woman you should only spend the magic moments of love. After that, spend the rest of the day with your buddies."
MARCELLO MASTROIANNI, ACTOR

"Hello, gorgeous. Could we discuss the possibility of rape?"
JOAN BAEZ, SINGER, ADDRESSING ACTOR DON JOHNSON

"March first if it's a boy. February twentieth if it's a girl."
GREG PRYOR, KANSAS CITY ROYALS THIRD BASEMAN, WHEN ASKED WHEN HE PLANNED TO REPORT FOR SPRING TRAINING (SINCE HIS PREGNANT WIFE WAS APPROACHING HER DUE DATE)

1987

> "What makes this marriage work isn't only love or sex. I need somebody called partner."
> **LIONEL RICHIE, SINGER, ABOUT HIS MARRIAGE**

> "It's time that people realize that women in this country can do any job that they want to do."
> **SALLY RIDE, ASTRONAUT**

> "Don't buy the garbage that you're over the hill at fifty. What I think is relevant is your experience, what you have to offer."
> **MOLLY YARD, PRESIDENT OF THE NATIONAL ORGANIZATION FOR WOMEN**

> "I play a busy woman trying to cope with a demanding career and a family at the same time. So what difference do a few extra pounds make in this day and age of so-called liberation and enlightenment?"
> **TYNE DALY, CO-STAR OF THE TV SHOW *CAGNEY & LACEY*, RESPONDING TO CRITICISM OF HER WEIGHT GAIN**

> "I was brought up to *do* something with my life, not to rely on a man or live through him."
> **DIANDRA DOUGLAS, DOCUMENTARY FILMMAKER AND WIFE OF ACTOR MICHAEL DOUGLAS**

> "It is not only a question of bringing women into the old roles of men but also of bringing men into the old roles of women. I believe that a better society will be created from this."
> **GRO BRUNDTLAND, PRIME MINISTER OF NORWAY**

1987

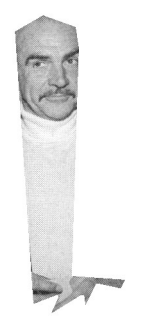

"I don't think there's anything wrong about hitting a woman. I don't, though, recommend hitting a woman in the way you hit a man."

SEAN CONNERY, ACTOR

"A three-point shot is like a woman. Sometimes you want to love it and sometimes you want to kick it."

BILLY TUBBS, OKLAHOMA UNIVERSITY BASKETBALL COACH

"Women tend to think that because eggs are coming, they have to build a nest. Guys aren't like that. We roam, we plant our seeds and move on."

GENE SIMMONS, ROCK SINGER

"If I could go someplace like Norway and find a seventeen-year-old girl, I'd be a happy man. I'd train her."

CORBIN BERNSEN, ACTOR

"Some of the better-looking ones here won't understand what I'll be talking about."

CHUCK YEAGER, LEGENDARY TEST PILOT, WHO BEGAN A TALK ON SUPERSONIC FLIGHT WITH A WARNING TO WOMEN

"Well, you always got Dolly Parton."

LARRY SPEAKES, FORMER WHITE HOUSE SPOKESPERSON, WHEN ASKED IF THE SUPERPOWERS WOULD "END UP RUNNING OUT OF TIT FOR TATS"

1988

"I consider the failure to pay child support a form of child abuse."
JIM MATTOX, TEXAS ATTORNEY GENERAL, WHO THROWS DELINQUENT DADS IN JAIL EACH YEAR ON FATHER'S DAY

"To rape the female lead twice in the life of the series is pure exploitation."
STEPFANIE KRAMER, ACTOR, THREATENING TO WALK OFF THE SET OF HER TV SHOW *HUNTER* IF HER CHARACTER, SERGEANT DEE DEE MCCALL, WAS RAPED AGAIN

"I'm not here [in Congress] because I'm a woman. Women are fifty-three percent of the population. We have some very important concerns."
U.S. REPRESENTATIVE PATRICIA SCHROEDER (DEMOCRAT, COLORADO)

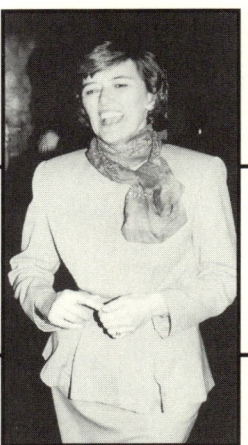

"A few years ago I would have said, 'I can fix him, I can make him better. All he needs is a . . . loving hand guiding him.' But now I'm curbing that impulse to try to fix somebody. I want somebody who's already ticking the way he should be."
SUSAN RUTTAN, ACTOR WHO PLAYS ROXANNE ON *L.A. LAW*, ABOUT WHY SHE'S NOT INTERESTED IN PLAYBOY TYPES LIKE HER TV BOSS, ARNIE

"I've never believed in chronological age. If you have health and energy, you have tremendous possibilities."
GLORIA VANDERBILT, FASHION DESIGNER

1988

"Physically fit, very attractive, and not too bright."
PAUL BLAIR, CHICAGO BEARS TACKLE, DESCRIBING THE PERFECT WOMAN

"I don't have to be there when the diapers are changed or [when] anything really awful happens."
WOODY ALLEN, MOVIE DIRECTOR, ABOUT LIVING APART FROM PREGNANT GIRLFRIEND, ACTOR MIA FARROW

"I'm so ugly I can't even get raped."
PHYLLIS DILLER, COMEDIAN

"Feminism is a failed ideology that produces women who are burned-out and bitter."
PHYLLIS SCHLAFLY, PRESIDENT OF THE EAGLE FORUM

"I've never been the type of woman that has to have equal rights. I've always been raised very old-fashioned. I don't want to have to take care of my husband. I want him to take care of me."
NANCY LOPEZ, PROFESSIONAL GOLFER

"I'm scared to death of money and . . . women. Those two things have caused more creatures' downfall than any other."
JIMMY SWAGGART, EVANGELIST

"That's like letting wives come between friendships. Friends are hard to find; you can find a wife anywhere."
MIKE DITKA, CHICAGO BEARS COACH, ABOUT BICKERING BETWEEN PLAYERS OVER WHICH ONE WOULD GET TO BE IN A COMMERCIAL

1988

"Maybe someday it won't be such a big deal when the networks hire a woman sportscaster. That would be a real sign of progress."
GAYLE GARDNER, NBC SPORTSCASTER

"There's a school of thought that it's really not very interesting whether a woman is married or not."
DIANE SAWYER, *60 MINUTES* CORRESPONDENT

"In any walk of life, the more secure two partners are in their individual pursuits, the better off the union is going to be."
DAVID LETTERMAN, TALK SHOW HOST

"You don't give up your right to an opinion just because you're married to the president."
NANCY REAGAN, FIRST LADY

"We've got women everywhere in this campaign . . . not because we set out to be half and half, but because we set out to get the best people, and half of the best people are women."
SUSAN ESTRICH, MICHAEL DUKAKIS'S CAMPAIGN MANAGER

1988

"Novels are like wives, you don't talk about them. But movies are different, they're like mistresses, and you can brag a bit."
NORMAN MAILER, AUTHOR, WHEN ASKED ABOUT HIS NOVEL-IN-PROGRESS, *HARLOT'S GHOST*

"If [Sugar Ray] Leonard and [Marvelous Marvin] Hagler were here today, I would walk up to them and slap them in the face. They deserve to be hit as if they were women—to make them think, 'Am I a man or a woman?' If they are men, they don't fight like men."
TOMMY HEARNS, BOXER

"I have six grandkids—four girls, though."
YOGI BERRA, HOUSTON ASTROS COACH

"Dirty socks."
JOHNNY DEPP, ACTOR, CITING A DISADVANTAGE OF BACHELORHOOD

"I knew I could strap a guitar around my neck and have girls lick my boot heels."
GENE SIMMONS, ROCK SINGER, ABOUT WHY HE CHOSE A CAREER IN ROCK AND ROLL

"I don't think you can have a happy marriage if you're constantly elbowing your husband and jockeying for position. His word is law around the house, and I respect his decisions."
DANIELLE STEEL, AUTHOR

1988

"I've always felt a little on the outside. I guess it's because I'm not the kind of guy who goes out and gets drunk three times a week. I'm not into hanging out in bars every night. I'd rather hang out at home with my wife. That doesn't make me a bad guy, does it?"

DOUG FLUTIE, FORMER CHICAGO BEARS QUARTERBACK, ABOUT HIMSELF AND HIS TEAMMATES

"When I'm old, I'm never going to say, 'I didn't do this,' or 'I regret that.' I'm going to say, 'I don't regret a damn thing. I came, I went, and I did it all.'"

KIM BASINGER, ACTOR

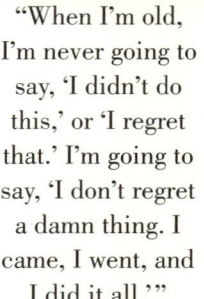

"I didn't like either one of my husbands. Why carry their names around? I don't want to be identified as Mrs. anybody."

CHER, ACTOR, ABOUT LEGALLY CHANGING HER NAME TO CHER IN 1975

"Remember, age is not important unless you are a cheese."

HELEN HAYES, ACTOR

"They used to say you married the man you wanted to be. Now you can be the person you want to be, and so you marry the man you want to marry."

BETTY FRIEDAN, WOMEN'S RIGHTS ACTIVIST

"I never want [my daughters] to see me as a victim. It's important for me that they see that whether I win or lose, I can always stand up for what I believe."

ESTHER SHAPIRO, TV PRODUCER

1983

"As far as our physical endurance and how our emotions change every month, I feel there are certain instances that we don't need to be in a place where a man is."
KELLYE CASH, MISS AMERICA 1987, ABOUT WHY SHE DOESN'T SUPPORT THE EQUAL RIGHTS AMENDMENT

"Girls should be like a good pitching staff. You've got to rotate 'em."
DENNIS HARRAH, L.A. RAMS GUARD

"These are women who are sort of pretending or trying to be men. They are sort of overcompensating for not being men. It's sad, you know, because it kind of doesn't work. . . . It kind of fights the whole wife role. Sure you got your career and your success, but you are not fulfilled as a woman."
ADRIAN LYNE, DIRECTOR OF THE MOVIE *FATAL ATTRACTION*, ABOUT CAREER WOMEN

"I don't have a cook except for the one I married thirty years ago."
JERRY FALWELL, FOUNDER OF THE MORAL MAJORITY

"She is saying 'Gaze upon my flesh. Don't I have a neat set of gams? Don't they turn you on?'"
MIKE ROYKO, SYNDICATED NEWSPAPER COLUMNIST, ABOUT WOMEN WHO WEAR MINISKIRTS

"It's not going to be a violent rape, where the guy rapes her and kills her. It's going to be a friendly rape."
MICHAEL PARE, ACTOR, TALKING ABOUT AN EPISODE ON HIS TV SHOW *HOUSTON KNIGHTS* CONCERNING DATE RAPE

1988

"One is responsible for one's own life. Passivity provides no protection."
MADELEINE KUNIN, GOVERNOR OF VERMONT

"Marriage could never mean giving up your own life simply to follow a man around. . . . Everyone has a right to a life of [her] own and interests of her own, and marriage shouldn't change that."
VICTORIA TENNANT, ACTOR AND WIFE OF ACTOR STEVE MARTIN

"I don't sit around thinking that I'd like to have another husband; only another man would make me think that way."
LAUREN BACALL, ACTOR

"I want to show people that limits exist only in your mind; that you can do anything you want to do if you put enough time and effort into it."
NANCY LIEBERMAN, LONG ISLAND KNIGHTS GUARD, THE FIRST WOMAN TO PLAY IN A MEN'S PROFESSIONAL BASKETBALL LEAGUE

"I'm not worried about getting older. I'm actually looking forward to it, to learning more, to becoming a better person. I think women should use what they've learned and totally revel in it."
KIM ALEXIS, MODEL

"The women who came West were as strong as the men. I treat women with respect in my stories."
LOUIS L'AMOUR, AUTHOR OF WESTERN NOVELS

1988

"I'm getting a divorce and dating a much younger woman. There's no way I can keep my wife and girlfriend happy at the same time."
TED TURNER, COMMUNICATIONS MAGNATE

"To demand equality between [a woman and a man] in any dirty work that stains her beauty and detracts from her femininity is unjust and cruel."
COLONEL MUAMMAR EL-QADDAFI, LIBYAN PRESIDENT, ABOUT EQUAL RIGHTS FOR WOMEN

"I believe Planned Parenthood right now is very heavily involved in sterilization as one of their means of birth control."
PAT ROBERTSON, PRESIDENTIAL CANDIDATE (REPUBLICAN), WHEN ASKED WHETHER OR NOT HE WOULD SUPPORT FEDERAL FUNDING FOR THE NONABORTION PROGRAMS OF PLANNED PARENTHOOD

"Some men simply don't feel comfortable with a woman wearing pants; the woman may unconsciously be threatening to her male colleagues. To me, this is reason enough for female managers not to wear pants in the office."
LETITIA BALDRIGE, ETIQUETTE ADVISER

"I think every woman wants to look up to a man, if she has any sense."

1989–1991

Whoopi Goldberg helped us bring our Attitudes page up-to-date in 1989 when she pointed out: "I am an *actor*. I don't understand *actress*. You don't call doctors 'doctoresses' or 'doctorettes,' you call them doctors." From then on, we've only had *actors*, *comedians*, *hosts*, and *Representatives* (rather than Congressmen and Congresswomen). Thanks, Whoopi!

Jay Leno also encouraged us by standing up to comedians who use put-downs as the basis of their humor. He says, "I don't make fun of women or do gay jokes, dirty jokes, or cruel humor. There's so much hatred and malice in comedy today. . . ." We agree.

And Barbara Bush inspired us with her New Woman attitude in 1990 but let us down a year later when she appeared on the "Thump" side of the page. She wasn't alone: several other well-known women did the same thing. Jane Fonda set a record by earning *both* distinctions in one year—1991.

Don Johnson receives his final Thump on the Head in 1989, after earning jeers in 1986 and 1987 too. We hope he's changed his attitudes—but we have yet to see him on the "New Woman" side of the page!

We laud several New Women more than once during these next few years: Whoopi Goldberg, the *actor*; Kim Basinger, another actor who may have earned a reputation for being difficult to work with but has only earned a reputation in *New Woman* for her liberated comments; and Ann Richards, newly elected governor of Texas and a "good old girl" in her own right. (Richards's opponent, Clayton Williams, made it all too clear why he shouldn't be elected in 1990 when he compared the weather to rape: "If it's inevitable, just relax and enjoy it." He deserves an *extra* Thump on the Head for that one.)

1989

"I told him I wanted to be recognized as a good driver, not a girl driver."
SHAWNA ROBINSON, RACE-CAR DRIVER, TO HER SPONSOR WHEN HE PRESENTED HER WITH A PINK RACING SUIT

"We're taught at a very early age to define ourselves through our partner and it leads to a lot of trouble. I think the most successful partnerships are when people define themselves and know who they are and respect their own needs and then come together because they want that companionship and that partnership."
GLENN CLOSE, ACTOR

"Early in the Reagan years there was speculation that Walter Cronkite would become [U.S. Information Agency] director and I would be his deputy. But this time, I'd [like to] be the head and he'd be the deputy."
SHIRLEY TEMPLE BLACK, FORMER AMBASSADOR TO GHANA

"I don't think it will hurt my career if people know I'm happily married. I think it's much sexier to be in love with your wife."
PATRICK SWAYZE, ACTOR

"Lots of people want to ride with you in the limo, but what you want is a guy who will take the bus with you when the limo breaks down."
OPRAH WINFREY, TALK SHOW HOST

"If she's good enough, I don't see any reason why she shouldn't be hired. There's a place in the National League for good umpires, period."
HAL LANIER, FORMER HOUSTON ASTROS MANAGER, ABOUT FEMALE UMPIRE PAM POSTEMA

1989

"I don't support wife beating but I understand it."
SAM KINISON, COMEDIAN

"I don't know what kind of doctor I am. But watching all these beautiful sisters here ... I'm debating whether I should be a gynecologist."
MIKE TYSON, HEAVYWEIGHT BOXING CHAMPION, AFTER RECEIVING AN HONORARY DOCTORATE FROM CENTRAL STATE UNIVERSITY IN WILBERFORCE, OHIO

"Isn't she the most beautiful maid you've ever seen in your life?"
DON JOHNSON, ACTOR, ABOUT HIS WIFE, ACTOR MELANIE GRIFFITH (MELANIE'S REPLY: "AND THE MOST EXPENSIVE, TOO.")

"I wish for less fiscal responsibility; in fact, I wish for *no* fiscal responsibility. I wish my father would win the lottery and give me a big allowance. I don't want to take care of myself any longer, and I wish this for other women, too."
FRAN LEBOWITZ, AUTHOR

"Femininity is goodness, tact, and weakness. Weakness and emotionality should be part of women—otherwise who are we, the rational and strong, going to defend?"
GEORGY GRECHKO, FORMER COSMONAUT, ABOUT FEMININITY

"I feel like a real woman for the first time. You need to have a man to be fulfilled."
DELTA BURKE ACTOR, ABOUT HER RELATIONSHIP WITH ACTOR GERALD MCRANEY

1989

"It can be a great idea, this concept of courage. It is the most important of all virtues, because without it we can't practice any other virtue with consistency."

MAYA ANGELOU, AUTHOR

"We have to reach a point where having a physical difference doesn't matter . . . I don't think anyone in my life judges me by the way my hands and feet look."

BREE WALKER, TV NEWS ANCHOR, ABOUT THE DEFORMITY OF HER HANDS AND FEET DUE TO A HEREDITARY DISEASE CALLED ECTRODACTYLISM

"I am proving in everything I do that blacks and women are as capable as anyone."

CONSTANCE BAKER MOTLEY, THE FIRST BLACK FEMALE FEDERAL DISTRICT COURT JUDGE AND THE FIRST WOMAN TO SERVE A FULL TERM IN THE NEW YORK STATE SENATE

"I love to go without it. Women have depended too much on makeup."

KIM BASINGER, ACTOR, ABOUT WEARING MAKEUP

"[My husband and I] badly want to have children together, but I'm almost forty, so there isn't much time. I just live each day as it comes. I don't believe in regrets. Just enjoy each other. Otherwise, you can spend an awful lot of time thinking, 'Oh, if we only had a child with us, or a family,' your mind convincing you that you are not complete the way you are."

SIGOURNEY WEAVER, ACTOR

1989

"Most top female executives I know are preoccupied with protecting their turf. Many relish their role as the only woman in the room. They'd rather be tokens than take other women along with them."

AL NEUHARTH, *USA TODAY* FOUNDER

"After you hit a home run, you get to be with the guys, and after sex, well, you know . . ."

D. B. SWEENEY, ACTOR, ABOUT WHETHER HITTING A HOME RUN IS BETTER THAN SEX

"I hope we're talking about the very young customer buying thigh-highs. I'd hate to see an inch of flesh showing on anyone over thirty."

BOB MACKIE, FASHION DESIGNER, ABOUT THIGH-HIGH STOCKINGS

"You don't build a company like this with lace on your underwear."

ADVERTISEMENT FOR *FORTUNE* MAGAZINE'S ARTICLE "AMERICA'S TOUGHEST BOSSES"

"If we wanted her to have a career, she wouldn't be having a child."

WAYNE GRETZKY, L.A. KINGS CENTER, DENYING THAT HIS MOVE TO THE L.A. KINGS WAS PROMPTED BY WIFE JANET JONES'S ACTING CAREER

1989

"I am an *actor*; I don't understand *actress*. You don't call doctors 'doctoresses' or 'doctorettes,' you call them doctors."

WHOOPI GOLDBERG, ACTOR

"I don't think to be professional I have to be more masculine. I'm not a very good imitation man."

BRIGADIER GENERAL GAIL REALS, THE HIGHEST-RANKING WOMAN IN THE MARINES

"Any woman who accepts aloneness as the natural by-product of success is accepting the punishment for a crime she didn't commit."

MARLO THOMAS, ACTOR

"Women, I think, get better as they get older. To me, what's attractive in a woman is reflected in the way she feels about herself. She may not be the most physically beautiful woman in the world, but she becomes attractive by the way she carries herself and thinks about herself—or doesn't think about herself."

TOM SELLECK, ACTOR

"I'd never consider her career as secondary to mine . . . I'm not the macho guy I play in some of my roles."

TOM CRUISE, ACTOR, ABOUT HIS WIFE, ACTOR MIMI ROGERS

"Sarah doesn't talk about needing her space and all that other garbage. She works seven days a week and still has time to make me dinner."
JAMES WOODS, ACTOR, ABOUT HIS FIANCÉE, ACTOR SARAH OWEN

"I liked his arrogance, his vanity. Arrogance is a privilege of men of his caliber. Not so with women. Arrogant women are a plague."
MARLENE DIETRICH, ACTOR, ABOUT ACTOR CHARLIE CHAPLIN

"I don't ordinarily allow anyone to use that 'Ms.' in this courtroom. What if I call you sweetie?"
HUBERT TEITELBAUM, FEDERAL JUDGE, TO PITTSBURGH ATTORNEY BARBARA WOLVOVITZ

"None of your business. I don't want to talk about it. I had my period."
PAT CASH, TENNIS PLAYER, WHEN ASKED ABOUT HIS DISAPPOINTING PERFORMANCE AT THE AUSTRALIAN OPEN

"My wife's married. I'm not."
CHARLES BARKLEY, PHILADELPHIA 76ERS FORWARD, TO A FEMALE PHOTOGRAPHER

"I still feel I could lose everything at any moment. But the greatest victory has been to be able to live with myself, to accept my shortcomings and those of others. I'm a long way from the human being I'd like to be. But I've decided I'm not so bad after all."

AUDREY HEPBURN, ACTOR

"I'm tired of the cliché of the dumb blonde, that if a woman is beautiful she has to be stupid. And I know a lot of women who are feminine, beautiful, bright, as good at their work as any man would be, or better, and I like to write about women like that."

SIDNEY SHELDON, AUTHOR

"Month by month I find my communication with women is improving. I think it's something to do with getting a little freer from the old roles—sensing one doesn't have to play them anymore."

JOHN CLEESE, ACTOR

"Honey, sex doesn't stop until you're in the grave."

LENA HORNE, SINGER

"It is really too bad that my mother and my aunts and my grandmother have been overshadowed by the men of the family, because they are impressive women who made the men what they are."

MARIA SHRIVER, TV JOURNALIST

"Just because someone's bigger than you, it doesn't give him the right to hit you. Women need to know that."

REBA MCENTIRE, COUNTRY SINGER, ABOUT SPOUSE ABUSE

1989

"If the men want to take off their jackets, feel free to. And if the girls want to take off their blouses, it's all right with me."

TED TURNER, COMMUNICATIONS MAGNATE, COMMENTING ON THE TEMPERATURE OF THE ROOM AT THE NATIONAL PRESS CLUB

"I'll be dead before Bo really starts to age."

JOHN DEREK, MOVIE PRODUCER, ABOUT THE SECRET OF HIS SUCCESSFUL MARRIAGE TO ACTOR BO DEREK

"I'm looking for a woman with an intense sexual appetite, because I don't ever want to have to cheat."

DAVID KEITH, ACTOR, ABOUT WHAT HE WANTS IN A WOMAN

"Women were created in a role of submission to men and should not be in a position of leadership."

BOB KNEPPER, HOUSTON ASTROS PITCHER, ABOUT FEMALE UMPIRES

"Australia is still a male-chauvinist bastion and most of the women like it that way."

PAUL HOGAN, ACTOR

"At some point these women were all normal little girls. Somewhere along the line they got sidetracked."

AL TRAUTWIG, ABC ANNOUNCER AT THE CALGARY OLYMPICS, OBSERVING THE NUMBER OF WOMEN PARTICIPATING IN THE OPENING CEREMONIES

1990

"There was no question that I wanted a child. There was no question that I could raise a child. And there was definitely no question that I hadn't met Mr. Right."

JANE WALLACE, UNMARRIED LIFETIME TALK SHOW HOST, ABOUT ADOPTING A BABY ON HER OWN

"I truly believe that one day Mount Rushmore will be coed. And it's about time. We have kept women down long enough."

BOB HOPE, COMEDIAN

"I don't draw bodies. You'll see heads, because that's where my characters' minds are. Women are always thought of in terms of their bodies."

BARBARA BRANDON, CARTOONIST

"It would be detrimental for me to compromise. I sing because of the way I am. I don't want to endanger my soul . . . because of my physical looks."

K.D. LANG, SINGER, ABOUT WHY SHE REFUSES TO LOOK MORE TRADITIONAL

"I must have been sleeping when my colleagues learned it would be much more difficult for us in business because we were women."

KARIN LOKAUG, THE UNITED NATIONS INTERNATIONAL CHILDREN'S EMERGENCY FUND'S TOP FEMALE EXECUTIVE

"There is still a stereotype that men are smarter than women, and I think that should be gone."

SUSANNAH BARKO-YOVINO, ELEVEN-YEAR-OLD WINNER OF THE NATIONAL GEOGRAPHY BEE

1990

"*L.A. Law* portrays its women lawyers realistically. In real life female attorneys tend to be overaggressive too. They generally lack a sense of humor; they're more defensive and have a misconception about what their male counterparts do. I can have a real fight in a courtroom with a guy and then be laughing with him ten minutes later. With a man you don't carry a grudge down the hall. You can't do that with a woman attorney."

MARVIN MITCHELSON, ATTORNEY WHO SPECIALIZES IN CELEBRITY DIVORCE SUITS

"Honey, maybe it's better that it's a boy because he'll be here to take care of you when I'm gone."

FRANK GIFFORD, SPORTSCASTER, TO HIS WIFE, ENTERTAINER KATHIE LEE GIFFORD, AFTER THEY FOUND OUT THEY WERE GOING TO HAVE A BABY BOY

"When I got to thinking, the way we get thoroughbred horses and thoroughbred dogs is through inbreeding. Maybe we would get a supersharp kid."

STATE REPRESENTATIVE CARL GUNTER (DEMOCRAT, LOUISIANA), ABOUT WHY HE BELIEVES INCEST IS NOT A VALID REASON FOR AN ABORTION

"I prefer girls who are young. When I eat a peach, I don't want it overripe. I want that peach when it's peaking."

JIM BROWN, FOOTBALL HALL OF FAMER

"I don't like aging. The only thing you get is wisdom. How many guys are sexually attracted to someone who is fifty years old?"

GRACE SLICK, ROCK SINGER, ABOUT GROWING OLDER

"She used to be a teacher, then she became a nanny. Now she's my nanny."

ERIC ROBERTS, ACTOR, ABOUT GIRLFRIEND KELLY CUNNINGHAM

1990

"I've always had the feeling I could do anything; my daddy told me I could, and I was in college before I found out he might be wrong."

ANN RICHARDS, CANDIDATE FOR GOVERNOR OF TEXAS

"One need not be married to achieve status."

MISS PIGGY, MUPPET, WHEN ASKED HER MARITAL STATUS

"There is no excuse for rape under any circumstances, and this law will make it clear that the victim of sexual battery should not be persecuted as the criminal is prosecuted. This new law is a major victory for the rights of crime victims."

BOB MARTINEZ, GOVERNOR OF FLORIDA, ABOUT A NEW STATE LAW THAT BARS RAPE DEFENDANTS' LAWYERS FROM CITING A WOMAN'S CLOTHING AS EVIDENCE JUSTIFYING THE ATTACK

"If I am remembered, I want it to be not just because I am a woman, but also because of what I have accomplished, and for the help I've given my people. That's what really counts."

WILMA MANKILLER, CHEROKEE NATION CHIEF AND THE FIRST WOMAN TO LEAD A MAJOR NATIVE AMERICAN TRIBE

"I don't think that your role as a leader is based on sex at all. Leadership is an individual idiosyncrasy, something that people have. It's from inside themselves."

KRISTIN BAKER, THE FIRST FEMALE CAPTAIN OF THE WEST POINT CORPS OF CADETS

"When I'm ready to stop [acting], you'll read it in the obituaries."

JESSICA TANDY, ACTOR

1990

"It means the end of a career. Everyone hates these women. Switch jobs and get revenge later."

LETITIA BALDRIGE, ETIQUETTE ADVISER, ABOUT WOMEN AND SEXUAL HARASSMENT SUITS

"Pregnant women are too confused to make a rational decision about whether or not to have an abortion."

U.S. REPRESENTATIVE CRAIG T. JAMES (REPUBLICAN, FLORIDA)

"I sport a caveman mentality. A woman should be a lady on your arm and a whore behind your door."

NIKKI SIXX, MEMBER OF THE HEAVY-METAL BAND MOTLEY CRUE

"Men will be staying on top where they belong."

DANNY DEVITO, ACTOR, ABOUT WHAT THE 1990S WILL BRING

"I know I'm fertile; I've got the checkbook to prove it. But getting a couple of girls pregnant probably gave me a sense that there's no sweat: I can have kids anytime I want. It seems like anytime I've ever wanted something before, I've always been able to obtain it. Plus, I've had the security of knowing I'm a proven performer."

GEORGE BRETT, KANSAS CITY ROYALS FIRST BASEMAN, ABOUT THE ABORTIONS OF TWO FORMER GIRLFRIENDS

"I've always maintained that there's a little bit of prostitute in all women. Or there should be. I think in order for a woman to be all that she hopes to be for a man, there has to be some of that there . . ."

SHIRLEY JONES, ACTOR

1990

"Somewhere out in this audience may even be someone who will one day follow in my footsteps and preside over the White House as the president's spouse. I wish *him* well."
BARBARA BUSH, FIRST LADY, DURING HER COMMENCEMENT SPEECH AT WELLESLEY COLLEGE

"I find the less you focus on [your flaws], the better off you are. Be yourself and be glad who you are."
MICHELLE PFEIFFER, ACTOR

"To absolutely love being a woman."
MADONNA, SINGER, WHEN ASKED WHAT SHE CONSIDERS THE ESSENCE OF FEMININITY

"I have a lot of respect for women. My policy is I don't make fun of women or do gay jokes, dirty jokes, or cruel humor. There's so much hatred and malice in comedy today and that makes me very uncomfortable. I think people—including comedians—get back what they give out."
JAY LENO, COMEDIAN

"We're trying to increase the number of women, so the foreign service is a very open field now. Women have been involved in wars and have been taken hostage. They've run the same risks as men, so why shouldn't they be part of a community that tries to make the world safer?"
THOMAS R. PICKERING, U.S. AMBASSADOR TO THE UNITED NATIONS, WHEN ASKED IF THE FOREIGN SERVICE IS A GOOD FIELD FOR WOMEN

"I'm a modern dad; I change the diapers. It's just common sense: why would someone else do it all the time? I'm not gonna break my arm by patting myself on the back because I change a couple of diapers. I'm looking forward to doing a lot of that stuff."
MICHAEL J. FOX, ACTOR

1990

"I'm a typical American male with a lot of bad feelings toward women that I work out in my characters."
ERIC BOGOSIAN, ACTOR

"If it's inevitable, just relax and enjoy it."
CLAYTON WILLIAMS, CANDIDATE FOR GOVERNOR OF TEXAS, COMPARING THE WEATHER TO RAPE

"I was there, and my son came right at halftime of the Bengals-Steelers game on *Monday Night Football*. There was a TV right in the room, and my wife cooperated well."
PETE ROSE, FORMER CINCINNATI REDS MANAGER, ABOUT THE BIRTH OF HIS LAST CHILD, TYLER

"She makes my bed every day, feeds me regularly, takes my messages faithfully, and puts my laundry in those little boxes tied up with ribbon."
TONY CURTIS, ACTOR, IN DESCRIBING THE HOTEL BEL-AIR AS "THE BEST WIFE" HE EVER HAD

"I'm pro-heterosexual. I can't get enough of women. I have sex as often as possible. . . . It's really hard to maintain a one-on-one relationship if the other person is not going to allow me to be with other people."
AXL ROSE, LEAD SINGER OF THE ROCK GROUP GUNS N' ROSES

1990

"I can't postpone my life until I lose weight. I have to live right now."
DELTA BURKE, ACTOR

"They were brought up by me with the motto 'Women can do anything.' I think for a woman just to use her looks and to be an actress or a model is sad—a woman should use her *brain*."
JACKIE COLLINS, AUTHOR, ABOUT WHAT SHE HAS TAUGHT HER DAUGHTERS

"I am not for abortion; nobody is for abortion. I am for your right to make your own hard choices in this world."
LINDA ELLERBEE, JOURNALIST

"*Feminine*—to me—is being strong and doing what you want but not being afraid to be affectionate. I'm a woman; I'm not ashamed or embarrassed or afraid of it. What *woman* means to me is gentle, sexy, and solid."
CINDY CRAWFORD, MODEL

"You know, of all the tough jobs I've had in my life, none has been tougher or more important to me than my job as a dad."
LEE IACOCCA, CHAIRPERSON OF CHRYSLER CORPORATION

"I am a pioneer, and sports is my frontier. It's been hard for a woman to be strong, fast, *and* feminine, but that's changing. I'm muscular, but that strength and endurance enhances, not diminishes, my femininity. I can wear six-inch nails and one-legged bodysuits and set world records. And leave a lot of men in the dust."
FLORENCE GRIFFITH-JOYNER, RECORD-BREAKING TRACK STAR

1990

"If you took off all your clothes and sat on my face, I might tell you."
PETER FREYNE, FORMER PRESS SECRETARY TO THE GOVERNOR OF VERMONT, TO A FEMALE REPORTER WHO WAS TRYING TO INTERVIEW HIM

"I'm very much in love with a woman, but I don't want her to know. If she knows I'm in love with her, she'll start treating me like s---. That's how women are."
ARSENIO HALL, TALK SHOW HOST

"You don't tell me how to hit, and I won't tell you how to make babies."
STEVE SAX, NEW YORK YANKEES SECOND BASEMAN, AFTER A FEMALE ART DIRECTOR SUGGESTED HE SHIFT HIS BAT DURING A PHOTO SESSION

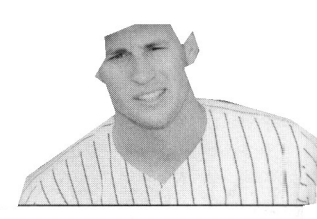

"Oh, where's the little woman? Where's the ball and chain?"
MIKE NICHOLS, MOVIE DIRECTOR, WHILE LOOKING FOR HIS WIFE, TV JOURNALIST DIANE SAWYER, AT A PARTY

"Radical feminism, of course, has vowed to destroy the traditional family unit, hates motherhood, hates children for the most part, promotes lesbian activity."
RANDALL TERRY, FOUNDER AND DIRECTOR OF OPERATION RESCUE, AN ANTI-ABORTION ORGANIZATION

"Do you know why God created women? Because sheep can't type."
STATE SENATOR KENNETH ARMBRISTER (DEMOCRAT, TEXAS) TO A FEMALE LOBBYIST

1991

"Being fat doesn't mean you feel good about yourself, but neither does being skinny."
ROSEANNE ARNOLD, ACTOR

"There will be obstacles; you may not have all of your dreams satisfied. But through a lot of hard work and believing in yourself, you'll reach the more important of your dreams. You just have to roll with the punches and keep going. Life, after all, has opportunity everywhere."
SUSAN WILLIAMS, THE FIRST NATIVE AMERICAN WOMAN GRADUATE OF HARVARD LAW SCHOOL

"I'm an artist; art has no color and no sex."
WHOOPI GOLDBERG, ACTOR, ABOUT BEING THE FIRST BLACK WOMAN ACTOR TO WIN AN OSCAR IN MORE THAN FIFTY YEARS

"Women really must have equal pay for equal work, equality in work at home, and reproductive choices. Men must press for these things also. They must cease to see them as 'women's issues' and learn that they are *everyone's* issues—essential to survival on planet Earth."
ERICA JONG, AUTHOR

"I'm happy to be the first woman, but I doubt I'll be the last."
GERTRUDE B. ELION, WINNER OF THE NOBEL PRIZE FOR MEDICINE, ABOUT BEING VOTED INTO THE NATIONAL INVENTORS' HALL OF FAME

"I do not know of a way to tell my five-year-old that I don't have time for her, that I have something more important to do."
TOM CLANCY, AUTHOR, ABOUT WHY HE DECIDED NOT TO RUN FOR THE SENATE IN 1992

"When I left Europe, my ideal woman was the one who . . . followed her husband. But I grew up and got reeducated here and understood the value of women doing their thing. It's an asset for a woman to have these qualities— you can have more interesting discussions, talk more intelligently with such a woman."
ARNOLD SCHWARZENEGGER, ACTOR

1991

"They can wiggle their waggles in front of her face as far as I'm concerned."

VICTOR KIAM, OWNER OF THE NEW ENGLAND PATRIOTS, ABOUT THE HARASSMENT OF A WOMAN REPORTER BY HIS PLAYERS

"I don't talk to people when I'm naked, especially women, unless they're on top of me or I'm on top of them."

JACK MORRIS, DETROIT TIGERS PITCHER, TO A FEMALE SPORTSCASTER WHO ATTEMPTED TO INTERVIEW HIM IN THE LOCKER ROOM

"It's a boy, just like I told her to have."

ANDREW "DICE" CLAY, COMEDIAN, ABOUT THE RECENT BIRTH OF HIS SON WITH HIS COMPANION KATHLEEN MONICA

"Now instead of going to the courts or getting a divorce, these women [currently being abused] will think, 'Maybe I'll kill him.'"

DENNIS WATKINS, PRESIDENT OF THE OHIO PROSECUTING ATTORNEYS ASSOCIATION, AFTER GOVERNOR RICHARD CELESTE GRANTED CLEMENCY TO TWENTY-SIX BATTERED WOMEN IN PRISON FOR KILLING OR ASSAULTING THEIR ABUSIVE PARTNERS

"I've got nothing against middle-aged women, but younger women are the only ones willing to give everything up and follow the lifestyle that I have."

PETER ARNETT, CNN INTERNATIONAL NEWS CORRESPONDENT, ABOUT PROPOSING TO A WOMAN THIRTY-THREE YEARS HIS JUNIOR

1991

"Over the years I have learned that what is important in a dress is the woman who is wearing it."

YVES SAINT LAURENT, FASHION DESIGNER

"We need more organizations to help these women, more shelters and better rehabilitation programs for abusers, because the problem won't be solved by just giving women a place to live. We have to get at the root of the problem and find a way to help the abusers, too."

MARJORIE JUDITH VINCENT, MISS AMERICA 1991, ABOUT HER PLANS AS A FUTURE LAWYER TO HELP BATTERED WOMEN

"People feel that if you look good and are also intelligent and capable of achieving career success, somehow that's not a particularly admirable combination. . . . This is the attitude that has kept women confined to certain narrow expectations for so long."

FAYE WATTLETON, PRESIDENT OF PLANNED PARENTHOOD FEDERATION OF AMERICA

"Age should *never* be a barrier to full participation in life. A good diet's important. Exercise is important. But what's most important is to *enjoy* life to its *fullest*, to do things for others, and to never, ever be afraid to stretch your limits."

SISTER MARY MARTIN WEAVER, SIXTY-FIVE-YEAR-OLD ROMAN CATHOLIC NUN AND WINNER OF FORTY-FOUR MEDALS IN A VARIETY OF ATHLETIC EVENTS

"When we as a society refuse to talk openly about rape, I think we weaken our ability to deal with it."

GENEVA OVERHOLSER, EDITOR OF *THE DES MOINES REGISTER*, ABOUT URGING RAPE VICTIMS TO SPEAK OUT

1991

"We do this because we want our guys to find us attractive."

JANE FONDA, FITNESS GURU, ABOUT WHY WOMEN WORK OUT

"Feminism was established to allow unattractive women access to mainstream society."

RUSH LIMBAUGH, SYNDICATED RADIO TALK SHOW HOST

"I think women force men to be unfaithful. Men are unfaithful by nature occasionally, but not as constantly as I was."

ANTHONY QUINN, ACTOR

"Listening to a woman is almost as bad as losing to one. There are only three things that women are better at than men: cleaning, cooking, and having sex."

CHARLES BARKLEY, PHILADELPHIA 76ERS FORWARD

"A woman carrying a Torah is like a pig at the Wailing Wall."

MEIR YEHUDA GETZ, ORTHODOX RABBI IN CHARGE OF THE WESTERN WALL, JUDAISM'S HOLIEST SHRINE

"I don't love women the way I love men. I love men pretty much. They're interesting. I'm more tolerant of them. I can say, 'Oh, he's an asshole, but I love him.' But if she's an asshole, she's an asshole."

DEBRA WINGER, ACTOR

1991

"I've always wanted a voice of my own. I have a great longing for self-fulfillment. I've never been able to sublimate those feelings. I could never be happy simply as a great man's lady."

KATI MARTON, AUTHOR, ABOUT BEING MARRIED TO PETER JENNINGS, ABC *WORLD NEWS TONIGHT* ANCHOR

"I hope one day you'll think I'm the smartest governor you've ever talked to!"

ANN RICHARDS, GOVERNOR OF TEXAS, RESPONDING TO A STATE BOARD OF EDUCATION MEMBER WHO TOLD HER, "I THINK YOU'RE THE PRETTIEST GOVERNOR I'VE EVER TALKED TO"

"Spend more time with older women. I happen to think women get better-looking as they get older."

ROBERT REDFORD, ACTOR, ABOUT THE PERCEPTION THAT WOMEN DON'T AGE AS WELL AS MEN

"How we treat each other is the core of all issues, and the relationship between man and woman is the most basic of human relationships. If we don't treat it with respect, I don't think we can solve anything else."

CORBIN BERNSEN, ACTOR

"It's never too late—never too late to start over, never too late to be happy."

JANE FONDA, ACTOR

"Motherhood and homemaking are honorable choices for any woman, provided it is the woman herself who makes those decisions."

MOLLY YARD, PRESIDENT OF THE NATIONAL ORGANIZATION FOR WOMEN

1991

"I don't screw around. If I'd done one third of what people say I have, if I'd had half the women, I'd be a *great* man. But I haven't. I wish I had."
DAN RATHER, *CBS EVENING NEWS* ANCHOR

"Why in God's name we're going to punish a man for having sex with his wife when she says, 'No, not tonight,' I don't know."
STATE SENATOR BUD LONG (DEMOCRAT, SOUTH CAROLINA), DEBATING A BILL ON SPOUSAL RAPE

"The *truth* is that women aren't interesting before thirty. Men are kind of *born* people."
JODIE FOSTER, ACTOR

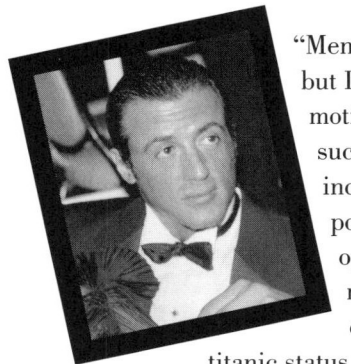

"Men may deny it, but I think their motivation to succeed, to be incredibly powerful and opulent and to maintain an overwhelming, titanic status in the community is for women. It is a sexual thing—it's done for either hands-on sexual gratification or for the sexual allure. Power. That's what women are drawn to."
SYLVESTER STALLONE, ACTOR

"How can we have an invasion when the troops storm ashore and then change their minds?"
BOB HOPE, ENTERTAINER, ABOUT WOMEN IN COMBAT

"If you can pick women, you can pick cattle. You look for good angularity, nice legs, and capacity."
BOBBY HULL, LEGENDARY CHICAGO BLACK HAWKS LEFT WING

1991

"I am not afraid to show my feminine side—it's part of what makes me a man."
GERARD DEPARDIEU, ACTOR

"It wasn't just a victory about makeup—this was about company prerogative and personal choice."
TERESA FISCHETTE, CONTINENTAL AIRLINES EMPLOYEE FIRED FOR REFUSING TO WEAR MAKEUP, AFTER GETTING HER JOB BACK

"I look forward to being older, when what you look like becomes less and less the issue and what you are is the point."
SUSAN SARANDON, ACTOR

"If all you have to offer is a look that is supposed to be appealing, then you are going to be paid attention to about a tenth as long as you would be if when you speak you are interesting."
JULIA ROBERTS, ACTOR

"Creating a civil rights remedy can never blunt the pain of a survivor of a sex crime, but it does say that we will not tolerate these crimes perpetuated against women simply because they are women."
U.S. SENATOR JOSEPH BIDEN, JR. (DEMOCRAT, DELAWARE), ABOUT THE RISING RATE OF VIOLENCE AGAINST WOMEN

"Women are learning that being assertive and feminine is not a contradiction in terms but one and the same."
DR. RUTH WESTHEIMER, PSYCHOSEXUAL THERAPIST

1991

> "You can't be president of the United States and also be a mother."

BARBARA BUSH, FIRST LADY

> "I feel he's a very normal guy. How else do you get a woman into bed?"

PATRICK BERGIN, ACTOR, ABOUT HIS CHARACTER IN THE MOVIE *MOUNTAINS OF THE MOON*, WHO LIES TO GET A WOMAN TO HAVE SEX WITH HIM

> "The only time I use them, they're either naked or dead."

JOEL SILVER, MOVIE PRODUCER, ABOUT WOMEN IN HIS FILMS

> "It is utterly ludicrous to think that women should even try to equal men; they never will, so of course women will have trouble getting to the top. They were not made for it."

BARBARA CARTLAND, AUTHOR

> "Feminists and all these radical gals—most of them are failures. They've blown it. Some of them have been married, but they married some Casper Milquetoast who asked permission to go to the bathroom. These women just need a man in the house. That's all they need. Most of these feminists need a man to tell them what time of day it is and to lead them home. And they blew it and they're mad at all men. Feminists hate men. They're sexist. . . . That's their problem."

JERRY FALWELL, FOUNDER OF THE MORAL MAJORITY

> "You know, it really doesn't matter what they [the media] write as long as you've got a young and beautiful piece of ass."

DONALD TRUMP, ENTREPRENEUR

> "The truth is no ugly woman can succeed in politics."

EDITH CRESSON, THE FIRST FEMALE PREMIER OF FRANCE

1992–1993

We've always felt that a woman has the ability to do anything she sets her mind to. In these next pages we hear from women who rap, drive race cars, fight for our country, and break Olympic records. As Katie Couric, co-host of the *Today* show, says, "A lot of little girls see me and say, 'I can do that.' I want them to see that I'm assertive, independent, and responsible." As these women break new ground, they pave the way for others to follow.

Women broke a lot of new ground in these next years. In fact, 1992 was dubbed "The Year of the Woman" because so many women were running for—and winning—political office. As Dianne Feinstein said during her Senate campaign, "Women are beginning to feel that they are not fairly represented. As we say, two percent may be fine for fat in milk, but not for the United States Senate." Hear, hear! And shame on Thumpee George Bush for saying that female Senate candidates were going to be easy to beat. (They weren't.)

In addition to the political races, look for quotes—both New

Woman and Thump—regarding the Mike Tyson rape trial, Anita Hill's charges of sexual harassment against Clarence Thomas, and the birth of a baby to TV character Murphy Brown.

Some of the spokespeople who emerged will surprise you. For example, George Foreman speaks out against fellow boxer Mike Tyson, in support of Desiree Washington. Madonna sides with Dan Quayle against single motherhood.

And it's always a surprise when couples appear on opposite sides of the page. Arnold Schwarzenegger and Maria Shriver offer contrasting viewpoints once again regarding "a woman's place." He blames working mothers for kids watching so much TV today—and earns a thump in 1992. And she sounds like a New Woman in 1993 when she says, "I didn't want to go . . . to being the wife of Arnold without ever having done anything on my own." Newlyweds Bobby Brown and Whitney Houston also seem a bit confused about their roles. He says he likes having a strong woman beside him. And she says women are "validated" by having husbands. It seems opposites do indeed attract.

1992

"I didn't want to leave the work I was trained for because of someone else's behavior. Why should we have to quit? Men assume we have choices that we don't have. And opportunities for women of color are even rarer."

ANITA HILL, LAW PROFESSOR, ABOUT STAYING AT HER JOB AT THE EQUAL EMPLOYMENT OPPORTUNITY COMMISSION AFTER ALLEGED SEXUAL HARASSMENT

"If one of them suffers because of the other, it's going to be the music that suffers. I'm responsible for what this child gives and takes to the world, next month and forty years down the road."

GARTH BROOKS, SINGER, ABOUT BALANCING HIS CAREER AND PARENTING RESPONSIBILITIES

"I was never a *victim* of the times I lived in. In fact, I was a success *because* of the time I lived in. My style of personality became *the* style. I was sort of the New Woman at a very early point."

KATHARINE HEPBURN, ACTOR

"Why when a woman enters the picture does sex enter the picture? Why does a woman represent sex? Why is it not power? Or strength?"

KATHY BATES, ACTOR

"She has supported me throughout my tennis career, through the difficult times and the nice times. Now, it's my time to support her. It's time for me to show I'm a real man."

KAREL NOVACEK, TENNIS PLAYER, ABOUT WITHDRAWING FROM THE OLYMPICS TO BE WITH HIS PREGNANT WIFE

"Women are beginning to feel that they are not fairly represented. As we say, two percent may be fine for fat in milk, but not for the United States Senate."

DIANNE FEINSTEIN, CANDIDATE FOR U.S. SENATE (DEMOCRAT, CALIFORNIA)

"Sexiness is no longer defined just as whether [women] are desirable, but also as what [women] desire. The more liberated women become—economically, politically, and personally—the more erotic we are. Freedom is a lot sexier than dependency."

NAOMI WOLF, AUTHOR

1992

"A smart girl is one who knows how to play tennis, piano, and dumb."
LYNN REDGRAVE, ACTOR

"If the wife comes through as being too strong and too intelligent, it makes the husband look like a wimp."
FORMER PRESIDENT RICHARD NIXON, CAUTIONING THE CLINTON CAMPAIGN ABOUT HOW IT USES HILLARY RODHAM CLINTON

"I'm sorry Miss Washington took it personally."
MIKE TYSON, CONVICTED RAPIST, ABOUT HIS ACCUSER, MISS BLACK AMERICA CONTESTANT DESIREE WASHINGTON

"There is a substantial and enlarging body of medical opinion that these deformities [small breasts] are really a disease."
THE AMERICAN SOCIETY OF PLASTIC AND RECONSTRUCTIVE SURGEONS, IN A MEMO TO THE FOOD AND DRUG ADMINISTRATION

"It is my legal judgment . . . that the testimony of Professor Hill . . . was flat-out perjury."
U.S. SENATOR ARLEN SPECTER (REPUBLICAN, PENNSYLVANIA) AT SUPREME COURT JUSTICE CLARENCE THOMAS'S CONFIRMATION HEARINGS

"Models are like baseball players. We make a lot of money quickly, but all of a sudden we're thirty years old, we don't have a college education, we're qualified for nothing, and we're used to a very nice lifestyle. The best thing is to marry a movie star."
CINDY CRAWFORD, MODEL

1992

"The women's liberation movement really had a profound effect on this whole country. I think you should call it a men's liberation movement because it liberated men, because it opened our eyes and our ears and our hearts. It liberated us from our own stereotypes. I think that the women's movement made men better."

A. M. ROSENTHAL, COLUMNIST FOR THE NEW YORK TIMES

"It was unbelievable to tell girls that being a prostitute after college while deciding on your career is okay because you'll meet your Prince Charming. It infuriated me."

DARYL HANNAH, ACTOR, ABOUT AUDITIONING FOR THE MOVIE *PRETTY WOMAN*

"I like a woman who is aware of her womanness in its universal form; a woman who isn't defined by what she's been told, or what she's been dictated to believe she's supposed to be."

WESLEY SNIPES, ACTOR

"Society's contrived image of what a woman should or should not be is something I've never agreed with."

LYNN HILL, THE NUMBER-ONE ROCK CLIMBER IN THE WORLD

" **S**he always was very independent. She knew how to work and provide for herself, which is what I loved. I love her and I never wanted to take her away from her independence. She still does what she wants, and I love for her to do that."

MICHAEL JORDAN, CHICAGO BULLS GUARD, ABOUT HIS WIFE, JUANITA

"You don't ask a man, 'Do you want to be in control [of your job]?' You *assume* he wants control. Why would a woman be any different?"

BARBRA STREISAND, MOVIE DIRECTOR

1992

"Why are you wearing this? I can't see your breasts."
OLIVER STONE, MOVIE DIRECTOR, TO A REPORTER WHO WAS INTERVIEWING HIM

"What a looker that one is. I wonder how many guys she had to sleep with before she got her BMW."
JAMES WOODS, ACTOR, REMARKING DURING AN INTERVIEW ABOUT A PASSING MOTORIST

"I don't think we should have to have them wandering the streets frightening women and people."
PATRICK BUCHANAN, PRESIDENTIAL CANDIDATE (REPUBLICAN), ABOUT WHY HE THINKS HOMELESS PEOPLE WHO AREN'T IN SHELTERS SHOULD BE LOCKED UP

"Women have been the slaves of men. Now they're less slavish. And sometimes to my way of thinking they should be a little more slavey. Then they'd have more fun. The relationships would work better if a man could protect and a woman could do her chore of making him feel great."
KATHARINE HEPBURN, ACTOR

"I finally got it right."
JACK NICHOLSON, ACTOR, UPON HEARING OF THE BIRTH OF A SON AFTER HAVING TWO DAUGHTERS

1992

"Self-esteem is the basis for feminism because self-esteem is based on defining yourself and believing in that definition. Self-esteem is regarding yourself as a grown-up."
SUSAN FALUDI, AUTHOR

"I'm really sick of people apologizing for feminism as if it would leave nasty stains. Feminism is one of the greatest humanisms. It's about making the world more human."
JODIE FOSTER, ACTOR

"I guess some people think we're weird, but my definition of femininity is what women do. If women choose to ride bareback horses, that's feminine behavior."
VICKIE CRAWFORD, WORLD CHAMPION RODEO BAREBACK RIDER

"If you give in to intimidation, you'll go on being intimidated."
AUNG SAN SUU KYI, WINNER OF THE NOBEL PEACE PRIZE

"It's easy for men to sit on the sidelines . . . while women have to make difficult decisions. I think people like Susan Faludi [author of *Backlash: The Undeclared War Against American Women*] are going to lead us to the answers."
DENNIS MILLER, LATE-NIGHT TELEVISION TALK SHOW HOST

"I feel very empathetic [toward] women who are asked to wear low-cut things. I've never had to act in a film where they said, 'Here, stuff this down your pants.' I think it's hideous, what women are asked to do and what they're asked to stand for in films."
BRUCE WILLIS, ACTOR

1992

"It ain't no big thing—I just threw her through a door."
ANDRE YOUNG, MEMBER OF THE RAP GROUP N.W.A., ABOUT THE CIRCUMSTANCES BEHIND A LAWSUIT AGAINST HIM

"I think prostitutes are generally happy about being prostitutes. It's not a bad way to make a living."
KEN RUSSELL, MOVIE DIRECTOR

"I wish that I was married and in a situation where having a child would be possible. People say, 'Well, have one on your own.' I say, 'Wait a minute, I'm not interested in raising a cripple. I want a father there. I want someone I can depend on.'"
MADONNA, SINGER

"Behind every feminist is either a ruined husband or a ruined father. Feminism is at its core dysfunctional."
RANDALL TERRY, FOUNDER AND DIRECTOR OF OPERATION RESCUE, AN ANTI-ABORTION ORGANIZATION

"Sex and violence go together like love and marriage."
PAUL SCHRADER, MOVIE DIRECTOR

"They say there's discrimination, so they revoke laws banning women from being truckers, construction workers, or miners. . . . Who wants to go home to a wife who smells of cement and has big muscles? [My wife] pilots the stove rather than a truck. That's more appropriate."
LUIZ CARLOS JACARO LADEIRA, FOUNDING MEMBER OF THE BRAZILIAN MACHO MOVEMENT

1992

"In a society where the rights and potential of women are constrained, no man can be truly free. He may have power, but he will not have freedom."
MARY ROBINSON, PRESIDENT OF IRELAND

"I don't know why it should surprise people women are so tough. What I do is probably not as tough as [being] a single mother, raising two kids, and paying rent or a mortgage."
LIBBY RIDDLES, FIRST WOMAN WINNER OF THE IDITAROD TRAIL SLED DOG RACE

"I had to fail to realize that self-worth isn't built upon one accomplishment. It's built through years of setting goals and reaching them."
STACY ALLISON, THE FIRST AMERICAN WOMAN TO REACH THE TOP OF MOUNT EVEREST, AFTER ONE UNSUCCESSFUL ATTEMPT

"It makes me sick when I hear people say [Desiree Washington] did this to get money, or that she was mad at [Mike] Tyson for rejecting her and this was her way of getting even. . . . No woman is going to subject herself to a rape trial for something like that."
GEORGE FOREMAN, HEAVYWEIGHT BOXER, ABOUT CHARGES BY MISS BLACK AMERICA CONTESTANT DESIREE WASHINGTON THAT SHE WAS RAPED BY FORMER HEAVYWEIGHT BOXING CHAMPION MIKE TYSON

"I'm proud [my hair] is completely gray, and I'm not going to bother with coloring it because I have other things to do with my time. Also, I like the way it looks. If it encourages other women to say, 'I can do that, too,' that's great, and they should wear it proudly. We earned those gray hairs!"
EMMYLOU HARRIS, COUNTRY SINGER

1992

> "[The fight for the E.R.A. in Iowa] is about a socialist, antifamily political movement that encourages women to leave their husbands, kill their children, practice witchcraft, destroy capitalism, and become lesbians."
>
> **PAT ROBERTSON, EVANGELIST**

> "It doesn't help matters when prime-time TV has Murphy Brown—a character who supposedly epitomizes today's intelligent, highly paid, professional woman—mocking the importance of fathers by bearing a child alone and calling it just another 'lifestyle choice.'"
>
> **VICE PRESIDENT DAN QUAYLE, ABOUT THE BREAKDOWN OF THE FAMILY STRUCTURE**

> "I said that eighty percent of the top one hundred [women tennis players] are fat pigs, but I overexaggerated a little bit. What I meant to say is that only seventy-five percent [are fat pigs]."
>
> **RICHARD KRAJICEK, TENNIS PLAYER, ABOUT WHY HIS FEMALE COUNTERPARTS DO NOT DESERVE PRIZE MONEY EQUAL TO THAT OF MEN**

> "All these femi-Nazis [feminists] out there, demanding their right to abortion as the most important thing in their life, never have to worry about having one anyway. Because who'd want to have sex with 'em?"
>
> **RUSH LIMBAUGH, SYNDICATED RADIO TALK SHOW HOST**

> "I was incoherent and radical. I was even a *feminist*, and I'm very embarrassed about it. . . . If you grow up as a Jew and a woman in New York City, you are a liberal until you go away and think things through."
>
> **LISA SCHIFFREN, SPEECHWRITER WHO WROTE DAN QUAYLE'S SPEECH ATTACKING MURPHY BROWN**

1992

"[I] can't imagine having a marriage that works these days without [the husband] doing the dishes or changing diapers."
TIM ALLEN, COMEDIAN

"They used to call up asking for a beautiful white model or a beautiful black model. Now they just ask for a beautiful model. [In modeling] it just doesn't matter what color you are anymore. If I've had something to do with that change, then I'm really proud of it."
NAOMI CAMPBELL, MODEL

"If the vice president thinks it's disgraceful for an unmarried woman to bear a child, and if he believes that a woman cannot adequately raise a child without a father, then he'd better make sure abortion remains safe and legal."
DIANE ENGLISH, CREATOR OF THE TV SHOW MURPHY BROWN

"We can only be a strong nation if we are a healthy nation—of men *and* women."
BERNADINE HEALY, M.D., DIRECTOR OF THE NATIONAL INSTITUTES OF HEALTH, ABOUT THE NEED FOR MORE WOMEN'S HEALTH RESEARCH

"One of the greatest social changes in my time has been the liberation of women, the movement of women out of a narrow number of jobs into much more of a broad participation in business. Women coming into the work force have done more to build the economy of the U.S. than perhaps anything else in the last twenty years."
JOHN H. BRYAN, CEO OF SARA LEE CORPORATION

"I don't believe makeup and the right hairstyle alone can make a woman beautiful. The most radiant woman in the room is the one most full of life and experience."

1992

"The only real meaning in life can be found in a good man. And maybe Paris. Preferably the two together."
MARILYN VOS SAVANT, AUTHOR, WHO HAS THE WORLD'S HIGHEST RECORDED IQ (230)

"I am delighted with some of the women that our [Republican] Senate candidates are going to be taking on because they will be easier to beat."
PRESIDENT GEORGE BUSH, ABOUT THE 1992 SENATE RACES

"The woman who agrees to hours of petting but does not want to complete the sex act is asking for trouble, and she will probably get it. The notion that a woman has the right to change her mind after two hours of passionate stimulation may be legally sound, but it flies in the face of the most basic facts of procreation and biological human drives."
ANN LANDERS, SYNDICATED ADVICE COLUMNIST, ABOUT DATE RAPE

"Menstruation and childbirth are an affront to beauty and form."
CAMILLE PAGLIA, AUTHOR

"I never imagined I'd be sleeping with a sixty-year-old woman."
U.S. SENATOR ALAN SIMPSON (REPUBLICAN, WYOMING), AT HIS WIFE'S BIRTHDAY PARTY

"It's harder to be sympathetic to the woman on welfare being interviewed on television when she's fat."
ANDY ROONEY, *60 MINUTES* COMMENTATOR

"I don't see TV as the villain. The villain is the economic situation and women's equal rights. Women go out and get jobs and the husband has a job . . . where does that leave the children?"
ARNOLD SCHWARZENEGGER, ACTOR, ABOUT WHY KIDS ARE WATCHING SO MUCH TELEVISION

1993

"We don't have gender laws preventing men from doing things. I personally believe gender-specific job criteria [such as restrictions preventing women from flying combat missions] are a mistake. The things that are important—such as courage, integrity, loyalty, luck, and determination—those things are not distributed on your chromosomes."

RHONDA CORNUM, U.S. ARMY LIEUTENANT COLONEL, WHO WAS A P.O.W. DURING THE PERSIAN GULF WAR

"Hollywood does not address the issue of stereotypes—about gays, about blacks, about women, about men, whatever—in a serious way. Then these stereotypical images end up on-screen . . . and the divisiveness becomes part of the culture."

JAMES WOODS, ACTOR

"I studied men and adapted myself to their world. I tried to emulate them. Eventually, I realized that I didn't have to 'become' a man to be powerful."

TWYLA THARP, CHOREOGRAPHER

"A lot of little girls see me and say, 'I can do that.' I want them to see that I'm assertive, independent, and responsible."

KATIE COURIC, *TODAY* SHOW CO-HOST

"Character contributes to beauty. It fortifies a woman as her youth fades. A mode of conduct, a standard of courage, discipline, fortitude, and integrity can do a great deal to make a woman beautiful."

JACQUELINE BISSET, ACTOR

"I feel that you reach a certain age and then things start to jell. My sense of self is stronger. I'm getting bolder in my old age. After I hit forty, you couldn't mess around with me so much anymore."

JULIE KAVNER, ACTOR

1993

"Why can't a woman be more like a dog, huh? So sweet, loving, and attentive."
KIRK DOUGLAS, ACTOR

"I think mothers kill instincts in children. Kids relate to violence in a completely different way. [They] have more fun with physical bopping than people give them credit for.... Anything that encourages children to be physical, to get them away from the mother thing, is good."
JOHN HEARD, ACTOR, ABOUT THE VIOLENCE IN THE *HOME ALONE* MOVIES

"Michael's not emotional. He doesn't take it personally if I correct him. And he never has P.M.S."
DANELLE BLACK, NBC EXECUTIVE, ABOUT HER MALE SECRETARY

"I think that brotherhood is a good thing, but what they've come to call sisterhood is merely an unhappy childhood raised to the level of a political agenda."
HUGH HEFNER, EDITOR-IN-CHIEF OF *PLAYBOY*

"Do you believe that their fathers and brothers will not take care of them?"
SUPREME COURT JUSTICE ANTONIN SCALIA'S REPLY AFTER BEING ASKED IF WOMEN'S CONCERNS WERE BEING ADDRESSED BY THE MOSTLY MALE COURT AND CONGRESS

"Women are supposed to have husbands. We are validated by that, and we validate ourselves that way."
WHITNEY HOUSTON, SINGER

1993

> "A dress is nothing. Fabric has no sex. Sexiness comes from the attitude applied."
>
> **GIANNI VERSACE, FASHION DESIGNER**

> "Arnold [Schwarzenegger] would always say, 'I can't make you happy. You have to make yourself happy and then we'll both be happy.' I didn't want to go from being JFK's niece, Joe's granddaughter, and the daughter of Eunice and Sarge to being the wife of Arnold without ever having done anything on my own."
>
> **MARIA SHRIVER, TV JOURNALIST**

> "I didn't think I was ever going to get married until I met Whitney.... It makes me feel better to know I have a strong woman beside me."
>
> **BOBBY BROWN, SINGER, ABOUT HIS WIFE, SINGER WHITNEY HOUSTON**

> "I think women now are admired for competing. I was one of the meanest competitors around. I had the coldness on the court, but I don't think it took away from my femininity."
>
> **CHRIS EVERT, FORMER PROFESSIONAL TENNIS PLAYER**

> "There are men over fifty on television reporting news.... And because they are wrinkled and gray, they have the appearance of being very experienced. It is time for television and our nation in general to stop this deluding fixation with youth and [to] respect the right of women to wrinkle and to [turn] gray—on the job. Sexism is a poison we have been drinking for too long."
>
> **BERNARD SHAW, CNN ANCHOR**

1993

"That woman that is suing [Mike Tyson] is a bitch. I don't care if he raped her . . . she should look at herself and look at the disgrace that she is making of women. Look at what she is doing to him by trying to get money off him, going around doing chat shows. She's used him, you know. It's disgraceful, and she's a disgrace to women. . . ."

SINEAD O'CONNOR, SINGER, ABOUT DESIREE WASHINGTON

"The vote of women for Clinton—greatly exceeding that of men—is being interpreted as a protest against Bush's pro-life position. My own guess is that much of that vote was maternal in nature. For many, Clinton emerged as a boyish victim of the chief of state, who was engaged in bullying tactics. A sense of fair play was aroused."

WILLIAM F. BUCKLEY, JR., SYNDICATED COLUMNIST

"Having a child is a choice and working is a choice. We shouldn't be subsidizing working mothers. I'd rather make sure the child's interest is protected."

GARY S. BECKER, NOBEL PRIZE-WINNING ECONOMIST, ABOUT WHY THE UNITED STATES SHOULD NOT HAVE A GOVERNMENT-MANDATED CHILD-LEAVE POLICY

"We're going to put you back in the fashion department."

U.S. REPRESENTATIVE FRED GRANDY (REPUBLICAN, IOWA), RESPONDING TO A QUESTION FROM A FEMALE REPORTER

"I never thought of myself as a boss. I'm just a chick singer."

WYNONNA JUDD, COUNTRY SINGER

"You'll never get fifty women to dress the same way in front of an audience of sixty-five thousand."

JERRY JONES, DALLAS COWBOYS OWNER, ABOUT WHY THERE WILL NEVER BE AN ALL-FEMALE PROFESSIONAL FOOTBALL TEAM

1993

"There are women who sit at home or hide themselves in unfulfilling jobs because they've believed stories that they're too dumb, too fat, too old, or too stupid to fulfill their dreams. I know because I bought into that long before I ever heard the term 'unconventional beauty.' What a frivolous issue beauty is. We mustn't be afraid to be ourselves and tell our stories."

KATHY BATES, ACTOR

"I realize that I live in a society where the words 'gentleness' and 'tenderness' have all but disappeared. We only celebrate people who show how tough they are and how big their biceps are, and so it's my duty to show something different."

PAUL COX, MOVIE DIRECTOR

"Empowerment . . . is not such a grand concept. Instead, it's about individual people doing small, everyday things to make life better. It's about the mother on welfare who gets her three children immunized, the young father who is not too tired to help with his son's homework every night. And it's about the person who practices safe sex, not once, but every time."

ANTONIA NOVELLO, M.D., SURGEON GENERAL OF THE U.S. PUBLIC HEALTH SERVICE

"Even more than the Pill, what has liberated women is that they no longer need to depend on men economically."

JANE BRYANT QUINN, SYNDICATED COLUMNIST

"Age is no barrier. It's a limitation you put on your mind."

JACKIE JOYNER-KERSEE, HEPTATHLON CHAMPION

"The show is the epitome of what I worked for since my first day in the business. Maggie doesn't use her looks or sexuality to get anywhere in life. She gets by on her strength of personality and her intelligence. I read her and I went, 'Yay! Finally! A real character!'"

JANINE TURNER, ABOUT HER ROLE AS MAGGIE O'CONNELL ON THE TV SHOW NORTHERN EXPOSURE

1993

"I don't cooperate with female reporters. They all ask me the same thing: Why is a man like me not married, and why am I still searching for the perfect woman? All they really want to know is why aren't I married to them."
MORT ZUCKERMAN, PUBLISHER

"It was Christmastime, and you know how women are at Christmas. You buy things and charge it."
MARGE SCHOTT, ABOUT HER PURCHASE OF THE CINCINNATI REDS

"They are trying to prove their manhood."
ROSS PEROT, FORMER PRESIDENTIAL CANDIDATE, ABOUT WHY HE THINKS WOMEN REPORTERS ASK HIM TOUGH QUESTIONS

"Duck feet? You're out. Pigeon toes? Out! Bowlegs, pimples, warts, moles, dark skin, scars, bad breath? Out! . . . [And] they must be virgins."
HAO YU-PING, DIRECTOR OF CHINA AIR'S FLIGHT-ATTENDANT SCHOOL, ABOUT THE AIRLINE'S REQUIREMENTS FOR FLIGHT ATTENDANTS

"The problem with Hillary [Rodham Clinton] is will she be treated like other cabinet members? Will she be able to take the heat like a man when the going gets tough?"
PHYLLIS SCHLAFLY, PRESIDENT OF THE EAGLE FORUM

1993

"In the beginning, cleaning and feeding a baby are the only two ways he can relate to you. A real trust develops at those very early stages: he's looking to you to sustain his life. Why anyone would want to miss out on that is beyond me."

TIM ROBBINS, ACTOR, ABOUT BEING A FATHER

"Not really, but my sister does."

ALBERT GORE III, AT AGE TEN, WHEN ASKED IF HE WOULD LIKE TO BE IN POLITICS LIKE HIS FATHER

"To me, that's what being liberated is really about—not being defined by one's relationships with men, but still being able to appreciate men on their own terms. Elaine can be part of the gang and still speak her mind as a woman."

JULIA LOUIS-DREYFUS, ACTOR, ABOUT HER CHARACTER ON THE TV SHOW *SEINFELD*

"When men do dishes it's called helping. When women do dishes, it's called life."

ANNA QUINDLEN, COLUMNIST FOR *THE NEW YORK TIMES*

"My definition of the word 'feminist' is a strong woman who looks out for her sisters, who would go out of her way to see another woman make it and who wants to build our self-esteem up as a whole. If we don't have any strong women in this world to back us up, then, you know, we're lacking what we should be stacking."

YOLANDA WHITAKER, BETTER KNOWN AS HIP-HOP SINGER YO YO

"Today's top drivers—like Michael Andretti and Al Unser, Jr.—were encouraged by their racing fathers to start at a young age. Exposure to the [racing] environment has to start early, and I'd like to identify and encourage [female] talent."

LYN ST. JAMES, RACE-CAR DRIVER

1993

"I think if a woman is seated next to a woman, she feels like she didn't get the best seat."
ALICE MASON, SOCIETY HOST, ADVOCATING THE TRADITIONAL SEATING RULE

"There are enough groups and people out there advocating safe sex. If it's not pertinent to the script, then I say, Why is it Hollywood's responsibility?"
MEL GIBSON, ACTOR

"We became friends again after a long period of no communication. . . . We were able to disagree as adults and not be, pardon the expression, like girls about it. You know, not so fragile."
RICHIE SAMBORA, GUITARIST FOR THE ROCK GROUP BON JOVI, ABOUT THE BAND'S FIRST ALBUM IN FOUR YEARS

"In order to do my best work, I have to have a strong household. I thought she would quit [acting] and then we would make our start as a couple."
TAKAHANADA, SUMO WRESTLING STAR, ABOUT THE END OF HIS ENGAGEMENT TO A POPULAR FEMALE ACTOR

"Every woman must take personal responsibility for her sexuality. . . . [A woman who is raped] must accept the consequences and, through self-criticism, resolve never to make that mistake again. . . . Rape does not destroy you forever. . . . It's like getting beaten up . . . men get beat up all the time."
CAMILLE PAGLIA, AUTHOR

"I'm quitting [the Olympic basketball team] for the swim team. I'm going to the pool as long as there are babes with no tops."
CHARLES BARKLEY, PHOENIX SUNS FORWARD

1993

"I know women who freak out over turning forty. They're always looking at their lines with a microscope. But I say, 'Honey, I've earned those lines. I'm here and I'm looking good.' . . . If a woman just tries to stay toned and beautiful-looking on the outside but hasn't developed anything of value on the inside, there's really not much to talk about."

DEBBIE ALLEN, ENTERTAINER

"Heart, courage, intelligence, and grace are the requirements. The bull doesn't ask to see your identity card."

YOLANDA CARBAJAL, ABOUT BEING A FEMALE BULLFIGHTER

"It will not be the year of the woman until we have half of the House and half of the Senate and a president once in a while."

GLORIA STEINEM, AUTHOR

"I'm convinced of two things: Every man should [help deliver their children] so they'd respect and appreciate women a little more. And, two, child care should be taught in high school to both sexes."

ROD STEIGER, ACTOR, AFTER THE RECENT BIRTH OF HIS SON

"There's already too many unrealistic role models for young girls, and for somebody to hear that Monica at 137 pounds is too heavy and should be pencil-thin, well, I think it's dangerous to play around with things like that. I know people who've had a problem with anorexia or bulimia. It's a serious illness. To be healthy is what's important."

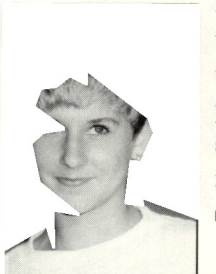

MONICA SELES, TENNIS PLAYER

"The sex drive of the male mounts and mounts and the female resists it, so his drive gets stronger and stronger. The 'no, no, no' is a biological thing that is a come-on to the male."

CARLETON ELDREDGE, ROCKINGHAM, NEW HAMPSHIRE, COUNTY ATTORNEY

"Madonna's the master [of self-promotion]. When *Malcolm X* comes out, I'm taking the belt from her. . . . I consider her a friend, and she sure knows how to work that publicity machine. Of course, I don't have breasts. If I did have [breasts], I'd be in the number-one spot over Madonna."

SPIKE LEE, MOVIE DIRECTOR

"[My triplet daughters' names—Kimmy, Kristy, and Kathy—] all start with a K because I struck out three times."

GARY ADAMS, U.C.L.A. BASKETBALL COACH, ABOUT WHY HE USED K, THE SYMBOL FOR A STRIKEOUT IN BASEBALL, FOR HIS DAUGHTERS' NAMES

"If he wants to still play tennis, it's a problem if his wife wants to go back to work. Somebody has to stay home and take care of the kids."

JIMMY CONNORS, TENNIS PLAYER, ABOUT JOHN MCENROE AND TATUM O'NEAL'S SEPARATION

"I've told Senator Zaffirini if she'll cut her skirt off about six inches and put on some high heels, she can pass any [bill] she wants to."

BOB BULLOCK, LIEUTENANT GOVERNOR OF TEXAS, ABOUT STATE SENATOR JUDITH ZAFFIRINI (DEMOCRAT, TEXAS)

"Our hookers don't do it out of obligation, of necessity. Here, prostitution doesn't occur for that reason, but because, somehow, they like it."

FIDEL CASTRO, CUBA'S PRESIDENT

Photograph Credits

AP/Wide World Photos: Madonna (page 8); Coretta Scott King; Cybill Shepherd; Vanna White; Oprah Winfrey; Mel Gibson; Corbin Bernsen; Woody Allen; Mike Ditka; David Letterman; Lauren Bacall; Katharine Hepburn; Patrick Swayze; Don Johnson and Melanie Griffith; Bree Walker; Wayne Gretzky; James Woods; Michelle Pfeiffer; Jay Leno; Steve Sax; Roseanne Arnold; Faye Wattleton; Debra Winger; Mike Tyson; Michael Jordan; Jack Nicholson; and Jodie Foster; **Ron Galella**: Gilda Radner; Shelley Long; Mick Jagger; Cher; Ivana Trump; Nick Nolte; Ryan O'Neal; Tom Cruise; Eric Roberts; Danny DeVito; Axl Rose; Delta Burke; Jane Fonda; Julia Roberts; Donald Trump; Diane English; and Kirk Douglas; **Globe Photos**: Linda Evans; Robert Redford; Cary Grant; Jerry Hall; Meryl Streep; Mr. T; Jimmy Connors; Anjelica Huston; Linda Ellerbee; Sean Connery; Patricia Schroeder; Johnny Depp; Danielle Steel; Kim Basinger; Glenn Close; D. B. Sweeney; Whoopi Goldberg; Paul Hogan; Frank Gifford; Florence Griffith-Joyner; Rush Limbaugh; Oliver Stone; Bruce Willis; George Foreman; Sharon Stone; Katie Couric; Whitney Houston; Bobby Brown; Sinead O'Connor; Wynonna Judd; Kathy Bates; Janine Turner; Ross Perot; Tim Robbins; Julia Louis-Dreyfus; Monica Seles; Debbie Allen; and Spike Lee; **Outline Press**: k. d. lang and Camille Paglia; **Neal Peters Collection**: Miss Piggy; **UPI/Bettmann**: Sophia Loren; Dudley Moore; Paul Newman; Julio Iglesias; Imelda Marcos; Ted Danson; Gloria Vanderbilt; George Hamilton; Angela Lansbury; Tammy Faye Bakker; Sally Ride; Betty Friedan; Jerry Falwell; Maria Shriver; Ted Turner; Arnold Schwarzenegger; Andrew "Dice" Clay; Ann Richards; Sylvester Stallone; Barbara Bush; Anita Hill; Madonna (page 69); Dan Quayle and George Bush; **Timothy White/Onyx**: Cindy Crawford.